Your Dollars, Our Sense

Your Dollars, Our Sense

A FUN & SIMPLE GUIDE TO
MONEY MATTERS

Karen Sarten, CFP®, Allison Hillgren,

Kelly DiGonzini, CFP®, Karisa Diephouse, Julie Johnson, CDFA®,

Commie Stevens, and Shannon Eusey

Your Dollars, Our Sense

A Fun & Simple Guide to Money Matters

Copyright 2017 Beacon Pointe Holdings, LLC

Disclaimer

ISBN: 978-1-946978-37-0

Acknowledgments

We would like to thank everyone involved in bringing this book to life, particularly our clients for their encouragement and confidence in us. We'd also like to thank Betsy Cooper, Hillary Huang, and Annie King for being our sounding boards. To our families and friends who constantly supported us through the development of this book, thank you for your feedback, perspectives, and truths. Without all of you, this would never have been possible.

Contents

About the Authors

Karen Sarten, CFP®

Karen earned her BA in Finance with honors from California State University, Fullerton, and maintains the Certified Financial Planner™ designation. Beginning with a college internship, Karen has spent her entire professional career in the financial services industry and joined Beacon Pointe Advisors in 2011. In 2017, Karen was voted Top 40 Under 40 by *InvestmentNews*. As a Senior Wealth Advisor, Karen is responsible for managing client relationships for Beacon Pointe's Private Client Services Group. Along with Beacon Pointe's Investment Committee Members and Financial Planning Department, as well as other key professionals, Karen is tasked with coordinating all areas of investment and finance to create and implement cohesive life plans for her clients. Karen's greatest motivator is knowledge. When she is not at the office, she enjoys traveling to new places and has become an avid podcast listener. She enjoys her close family and is looking forward to starting one of her own, soon. Karen currently resides in Newport Beach, California.

Allison Hillgren

Allison (Alli) graduated from the Marshall School of Business at the University of Southern California where she was captain of the Division

1, Pac-12, USC women's volleyball team. She also received a Master in Communication Management (MCM) from the Annenberg School of Communication and Journalism at USC. Alli joined Beacon Pointe Advisors in 2010 and oversees the firm's Marketing and Communications Department. Her responsibilities include website oversight, presentation and video development, social media and content management, and market research. Outside of the office, Alli volunteers her time working with her family's non-profit organization, The Patriots Initiative. She also enjoys horseback riding, golfing, traveling, and spending time with family. Alli is engaged to be married and currently resides in Newport Beach, California.

Kelly DiGonzini, CFP®

Kelly graduated from Gonzaga University School of Business with a concentration in Business Law. She earned her Master of Science in Taxation (MST) degree from William Howard Taft University, focusing on the taxation of partnerships, estate taxation and planning, income taxation of estates and trusts, tax aspects of charitable giving, and the taxation of real estate. Kelly received her Personal Financial Planning certification from the University of California, Irvine, and maintains the Certified Financial Planner™ designation. Kelly joined Beacon Pointe Advisors in 2012 and is responsible for helping the firm's private clients determine and meet their financial and estate planning goals. Prior to joining Beacon Pointe Advisors, Kelly spent four years doing financial planning at MetLife for individuals and small business owners. Kelly's writings about  various tax and financial planning topics have appeared in multiple publications, including the Financial Planning Association, *Elite Daily*, *LifeHealthPro*, *MainStreet!*, and *Financial Advisor IQ*. Her hobbies include bike-riding, yoga, tennis, and spending time with friends and family. She is also a member of the Financial Planning Association of Orange County. Kelly currently resides with her husband in Newport Beach, California.

Karisa Diephouse

Karisa earned her BS in Finance from California State University, Long Beach. Beginning with a part-time job in college, Karisa has spent her entire professional career in the financial services industry and joined Beacon Pointe in 2014. As Director of Partnership Integration and Strategy, Karisa works with the Beacon Pointe Wealth Advisor partner offices as a consultant on office growth and improving operational efficiencies. When new offices partner with Beacon Pointe, Karisa is the project manager for the merger and is instrumental to connecting them to the Beacon Pointe philosophy and culture. Formerly, Karisa worked directly with individual clients advising them on wealth management strategies to match their life goals. When she is not in the office, she enjoys taking long walks to the park with her kids, traveling, running and spending time with her family and friends. Karisa currently resides with her husband and two sons in Mission Viejo, California.

Julie Johnson, CDFA®

Julie earned her BS in Marketing from San Diego State University and maintains the Certified Divorce Financial Analyst® designation. Julie joined Beacon Pointe Advisors in 2010, and as a Senior Wealth Advisor, Julie is responsible for managing client relationships for Beacon Pointe's Private Client Services Group. Prior to joining Beacon Pointe, Julie was a Retirement Income Specialist with AIG Sun America, and prior to that she was with MetLife. She is very focused on helping clients meet their retirement goals and working through major life transitions. Outside of work, she enjoys running, playing golf, and spending time with family. Julie and her husband live with their two children in Ladera Ranch, California.

Commie Stevens

Commie earned her Juris Doctor from Pepperdine University School of Law and her BA in Economics from the University of California at Irvine. She is a member of the State Bar of California and an Investment Advisor Representative. Commie designed and oversees Beacon Pointe's approach to financial and estate planning. She works closely with individuals and their families to best utilize their wealth to meet their lifetime and legacy goals. Prior to joining Beacon Pointe Advisors in 2009, Commie practiced as an estate planning attorney at Albrecht & Barney and served as the Director of Estate Planning for Pacific Life Insurance Company. She has been featured in the *Wall Street Journal, US News & World Report, The Street, Financial Advisor IQ,* The National Financial Educators Council, the *Journal of Practical Estate Planning,* and *UCI's Wealth Management Frontier Journal.* Commie is passionate about financial education and regularly speaks on a host of financial and estate planning topics and has been a guest lecturer at Stanford University and the Paul Merage School of Business at the University of California at Irvine. Commie enjoys spending time with her husband and two daughters and resides in Laguna Niguel, California.

Shannon Eusey

 Shannon graduated with a BA in Social Science from the University of California, Irvine, where she played Division I volleyball. She received her MBA from the University of California, Los Angeles, Anderson School of Management. Shannon is Chief Executive Officer of Beacon Pointe Advisors and a member of Beacon Pointe's Investment Committee. Prior to founding and launching Beacon Pointe Advisors in 2002, Shannon served as Senior Managing Director and Portfolio Manager at Roxbury Capital Management and oversaw the socially responsible investments (SRI) for several years. Shannon is also a member of the CNBC Financial Advisor Council and is very passionate about financial education. Shannon serves on the board of the Young Presidents Organization (YPO) for the Orange County chapter, serves on the UCI Athletic Fund Board, and is currently an adjunct professor for the UCI Paul Merage School of Business. Shannon resides with her husband and four children in Newport Beach, California.

Your Dollars, Our Sense

A FUN & SIMPLE GUIDE TO

MONEY MATTERS

Chapter 1
Financial Essentials

We asked ourselves, "What are the finance essentials that readers must know?" Ultimately, we settled on five areas of personal finance with which we believe every person should be familiar. Like a great wardrobe, some parts of personal finance are essential and others are more like accessories. It's only when the outfit is complete that you truly feel put together.

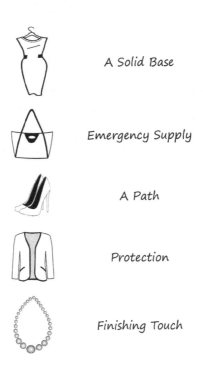

A Solid Base

Emergency Supply

A Path

Protection

Finishing Touch

[1]
The Base Layer—Prioritizing Spending

Every great outfit starts with a solid base—a classic, A-line dress; flattering jeans; or the perfect white T-shirt. All other wardrobe decisions—shoes, handbag, accessories—will be shaped around this base layer. Consider a **budget** to be your "financial base" and the first layer of your financial wardrobe. Your budget is the foundation from which all other financial decisions will be made.

Of course, we understand that creating a budget and choosing a blouse are completely different in practice, but they are both about planning and control. You get to say what goes! Approach budgeting as a way to see and to take control of your spending. Not knowing where your money is going is much more stressful than choosing the right outfit. Sticking to a budget will reduce stress and help you stay focused on the things that are important to you.

If you are just starting out, we recommend sticking to the 50/30/20 rule of thumb; allocate 50% of your after-tax income to your needs (such as housing and groceries), 30% to wants (vacations, daily lattes, and Netflix), and 20% to savings and/or paying off debt.

If you are in your forties or older, be sure to check out Entry #24: Image Isn't Everything to see if your savings are on track.

[2]
The Clutch—Planning for Emergencies

Solid base, *check!* Now, you can add other pieces to your wardrobe. While you might be feeling fabulous already, you're not ready to leave the house just yet. Before venturing out for the day, you'll want to be prepared for the what-ifs. What if you get a headache? What if your child gets a runny nose? What if you need an extra hat rack (or plant or floor lamp)? Okay, so Mary Poppins might have overdone it, but she and her magic bag were on the right track in terms of preparing for the unexpected. Consider an *emergency fund* to be your financial handbag. You fill it up, just in case.

Redirect 20% of your paycheck to a savings account, until you have stashed away enough cash to cover three to six months of expenses. Traditionally, the rule of thumb was to set aside enough to cover your *essential* expenses, like housing, food, and utilities. Instead, consider establishing a reserve to cover *all* your living expenses, as the line between essential and discretionary can become blurry during a financial hardship. (Vino, anyone?) Even when interest rates on cash are low, the value it can provide in a crunch—compared to say, charging on a high-interest credit card—might far exceed lost earnings.

[3]
The Path—Saving for Your Future

Your fashion sense is improving with a great base layer and an emergency stash. But, no outfit would be complete without a killer pair of heels. Before stepping out, you must decide what heel to step into. Consider a savings plan as your financial heel; it supports you on your path for life and, if chosen well, will get you where you're going faster. In the words of famous shoe designer Christian Louboutin, "A shoe has so much more to offer than just to walk."

Just as the right pair of heels depends on a number of factors, such as occasion, weather, mood, and (let's be honest) pedicure status, there are many factors to consider when choosing a savings vehicle, and you will likely end up with more than just one. As you save for multiple goals, like your first house, retirement, or college, savings vehicles might include Individual Retirement Arrangements (IRAs), 401(k)s, other retirement plans, and nonretirement investment accounts. Which account type to choose will depend on a number of factors that are unique to your situation (more in Chapter 5: Retirement).

Aim to save 20% of your take-home pay. Work with your financial advisor to develop a savings strategy that considers your goals, timeframe, tax situation, employer contributions, etc.

[4]
The Blazer—Protecting Your Valuables

Now that you have the basic money essentials—a solid base layer (budget), a piece for the what-ifs (emergency fund), and support for where you're going (savings plan)—there are just a couple of items left to complete your financial collection. Because no one likes to get stuck in the cold, it's wise to work a blazer option into every outfit. Consider *insurance* to be your financial blazer; it travels light and you will be glad to have the protection if you need it. Insurance can protect you from the loss of income and the assets you have to show for such hard-earned income.

Your financial closet just isn't in order if you don't have these forms of protection:

Health Insurance: Regardless of the current legal requirements, minimally having health insurance to protect your assets, in case of large healthcare costs, is vital to being financially buttoned up.

Life Insurance: If you have loved ones who depend on your income, we recommend having enough life insurance so that the investment growth alone could replace your after-tax income, leaving the principal available for large or unexpected expenses, in addition to a cushion for lower-than-expected market returns. Additional coverage might also be purchased to pay off existing debts or to fund other large future outflows, such as college. Eventually, your insurance needs are likely to decrease as your debts are paid down and future earning years become less. Fortunately, *term life insurance*, commonly used to cover your income replacement needs, is affordable.

Long-Term Disability Insurance: While most people understand the need to replace income if they pass away, they often forget to replace that income for themselves or loved ones if they become disabled. This is a critical mistake, because you are at greater risk of becoming disabled than of dying. Disability insurance generally replaces 50%–70% of income, should you become unable to work due to sickness or injury. Group disability insurance is often available through employment (and fairly affordable), with most plans providing a percentage of income, up to a maximum dollar amount. Be sure to know what the maximum benefit is so you can determine if it is sufficient for your needs. A supplemental individual policy should be purchased to cover any estimated shortfall.

Personal Liability (Umbrella) Insurance: Liability insurance protects existing assets and future income from the risk of liabilities imposed by lawsuits or other similar claims. Underinsuring for a potential liability is one of the most common money missteps. An umbrella policy adds an extra layer of protection when claims exceed the limits provided under traditional auto and homeowners policies (typically $100,000–$300,000). The common rule of thumb is to obtain an umbrella policy equal to the amount of your net worth, which is surprisingly inexpensive.

[5]
The Finishing Touch—Communicating Your Wishes

Take a step back, look in the mirror and prepare yourself to take one final step toward financial completeness. Next up, accessories! In the words of fashion designer Oscar de la Renta, "A woman makes an outfit her own with accessories."

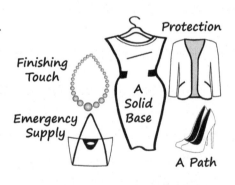

Consider an estate plan to be your financial accessory; it's your unique way of expressing yourself, yet it's easy to overlook.

Think of an estate plan as your playbook for what happens after your incapacitation or passing. It's an important financial accessory, yet most Americans do not have one. Whether it's avoiding the unpleasant thoughts, or the idea that you are too young or not wealthy enough to need one, no excuse will matter if the unexpected occurs. While sometimes a single statement necklace is all an outfit calls for, you will need more than one document to handle issues that arise from incapacity or death. Refer to Chapter 8: Estate Planning for a complete list of key estate planning documents and considerations.

With this finishing touch, your look is complete! You can head out for the day looking great and feeling confident.

[6]
How Do I Look?—Keeping Up with Credit

Now, we know you look great, but how you look on paper also matters. Lenders, insurers, and employers are all checking your credit, so here are our top tips to make sure you're putting your best financial self forward.

Take a look. Recognize yourself? Take 10 minutes and log onto <u>Annualcreditrreport.com</u> to review your free report from each of the major credit reporting agencies (Equifax, Experian, and TransUnion). While the free version won't get you your actual score, the report might reveal damaging errors or potential fraud. If you find an error, first, take a deep breath and put your patience pants on.

Next, write a dispute letter to the reporting creditor and notify all three reporting agencies (in writing) of your dispute. You might also need to notify other agencies, like your bank or investment firm, the Internal Revenue Service (IRS) or the U.S. Social Security Administration if you have fallen victim to identify theft. For more information and guidance, we recommend Myfico.com.

Ultimately, how good you look from a credit standpoint is "graded" by your **FICO score**, named for the company (Fair Isaac Corporation) that calculates the score. Each major reporting agency has a different formula, so your score will vary from one to the other. We guess you could say that credit beauty is in the eye of the reporter! Fortunately, the factors affecting your credit are consistent, and there are steps you can take to improve your score with all three agencies.

Our advice to looking your credit best is to pay every bill on time, pay off (in full) your credit cards monthly, and avoid charging more than one-third of your available credit limit. You'll also want to avoid opening too many cards and steer clear of tempting 0% store financing plans, which are viewed as "credit of last resort."

Two $ense

Generally speaking, an excellent credit score is above a 720; a good credit score ranges from 690 to 719. Anything less than a 689 is a credit score that needs improving. The average FICO score in 2017 was 699.

Generally, your score is weighted as follows:

35%— payment history (the timelier, the better)

30%— amount of debt you owe (less is more)

15%— length of credit history (the longer, the better)

10%— new credit inquiries (fewer is better)

10%— ability to manage different types of credit (mortgage/rent, credit card, etc.)

End of Chapter Resources

Personal Spending Worksheet
Sample Credit Report Dispute Letter of Explanation

To access the end of chapter resources, go to
www.GetTheSense.com/Book-Resources.

Chapter 2

Saving and the Power of Compounding

As advisors, one of the most common questions we hear is, "What investment should I buy?" This question is a little like asking your doctor for a prescription before he or she has had a chance to check your vitals. Think of saving as your financial vitals. A professional will want to ensure that you are financially healthy before recommending an investment. Your savings rate and the amount you have saved are the strongest indicators of financial health. While investing is important, *saving is more important*. Saving is also more challenging and, like blood pressure, it is hard to remember what's good and what's not. In this chapter, we will help you assess your financial vitals and hopefully motivate you to lead a healthier financial life.

[7]
A Drop in the Buckets—Healthy Saving Habits

We get it. You haven't created a budget, because you had to go to your friend's dog's birthday party. Feel free to insert your additional excuses here. Budgeting does not necessarily mean that you have to spend less. It's about knowing where your money is going, and knowledge is power. Once you identify your money trail, you will know if you are staying true to your financial values.

We'll make it simple. An easy way to see if your spending habits are healthy is to take stock of what you are saving. Include savings toward 401(k)s or other employer plans, IRAs, investment accounts, bank savings, and/or anywhere else you might be socking money away. If you are saving at least 20% of your *after*-tax income, then your current spending habits are healthy.

Not saving 20%? Don't panic. It's just time to take a closer look at how you are spending your money. Consider using an expense tracker to help capture everything. Or, look into budgeting tools to track and categorize your spending. Then, organize your expenses into two categories: *needs* and *wants*. Consider your "needs" to be expenses that cannot be avoided and are essential to your basic needs. Everything else is a "want."

If you're like most people, your allocation toward "wants" might surprise you, and there are likely simple changes that will go a long way. If nothing else, knowing how you have been spending will make you more aware of mindless credit card swipes and your spending habits will start to change. If you are overspending on needs, take a look at what might be eating into your retirement nest egg (for example, housing and/or car expenses) and what adjustments can be made.

Saving 20%? Before enjoying that next splurge, check to see if your cumulative savings are on track. After all, your current spending will not reflect your previous habits, but your nest egg will. To see if you're on track (to not have to work forever), refer to Entry #24: Image Isn't Everything. If your cumulative savings are not on track, work with your financial advisor or use an online calculator to determine how much more you will need to save to catch-up.

Saving 20% and the nest egg is on track? Well done! Just be sure to avoid sneaky little lifestyle creep. In other words, don't let your lifestyle grow in exact proportion to your income. Rather than spending more with salary increases or bonuses, save them! Consider this: Receiving a $3,000 after-tax raise in your thirties could add up to more than $350,000 in savings (assuming a 6.5% return).

GROSS INCOME (BEFORE TAXES*)
- Federal Income
- State Income Tax
- FICA Tax
- State Disability*

= AFTER-TAX INCOME

NEEDS 50% AFTER-TAX INCOME
WANTS 30% AFTER-TAX INCOME
SAVINGS 20% AFTER-TAX INCOME

* If Applicable

[8]

Smarter than Your Smartphone—
The Power of Compounding

Uber, Venmo, Mint . . . innovation is making our financial lives easier than ever. But the single most valuable financial invention—one that physicist Albert Einstein supposedly called the most important invention of all time—won't be found on your smartphone. We're talking about the *power of compounding*.

Compounding refers to generating earnings on your initial investment *and* on earnings the investment has previously made. Compounding can turn a small investment into a large sum, but time is of the essence. The earlier you start saving, the more compounding can work its magic.

Want to be a millionaire by age 65? Assuming a 5% annual rate of return, you can reach millionaire status by saving $8,000 per year starting at age 25. If you wait until age 35, you will instead need to almost double your savings to about $14,000 per year. In other words, saving earlier allows you to save less. So, save early and save often. Your future self will thank you!

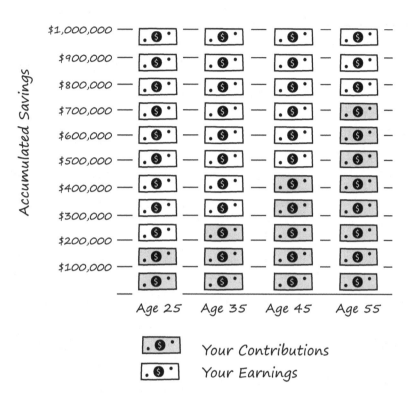

"Someone is sitting in the shade today because someone planted a tree a long time ago."

—Warren Buffett

[9]
Latte-Dah—Compounding Made Easy

Next time you rush to the local coffee shop for your caffeine fix, remember that the power of compounding makes a big difference. Consider this: the daily $3.60 cost of a medium-sized latte will run you $1,300 per year. And, we're not talking fancy drinks here, just coffee and milk (and just one a day)! If, instead, you redirected the $109 a month toward savings, assuming a 5% rate of return, the accumulation potential is major.

Investment Time	Value Just Over
15 years	$31,000
20 years	$50,000
30 years	$109,000

Ok, we're reading your thoughts . . . *If I don't have caffeine, I don't work. If I don't work, I don't make money. If I don't make money, I don't save money.* We get it. We love those warm little cups with our misspelled names just as much as you do. We aren't trying to stage an intervention here. Our point is that it's important to look at the annual cost of small indulgence so that you can mindfully decide whether your dollars are going toward what's really important to you or not.

If not coffee, consider other ways to cut back—perhaps something that won't cause such nasty withdrawals!

[10]
Time for a Stretch—Saving through Seasons

Whether it's getting beach bods ready for summer or the New Year's resolution-goers trying to get rid of the unwanted holiday weight, there are times during the year when a packed gym makes it hard for you to do your walking lunges. Just as there are seasons when a herd at the gym will make it hard to get in a good stretch, there are times in life when a crowd of financial responsibilities can make it hard to stretch your paycheck. Not to worry, there will be lulls in gym-going activity and times in your life when you will have more *discretionary income* to save.

Discretionary income is the amount of income leftover after taxes and after paying for the basic necessities in life; it is the pool from which you save. Even though your income is likely to be lower in your twenties and early thirties, less of it will be allocated toward necessary expenses at this point in life, leaving more room for saving. Be sure to maximize your opportunity to save during this time.

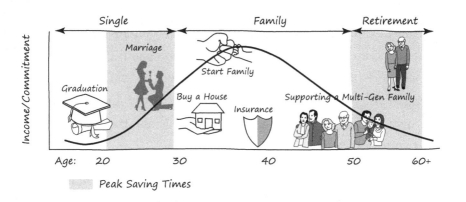

In your mid-thirties and forties, you will have little discretionary income as life happens. Kids, mortgage, new car, more groceries, additional insurance needs—you get the picture. This is the time when saving seems impossible. Don't beat yourself up. Save what you can.

Usually, in your fifties and sixties, kids are grown, college is a memory, the mortgage is close to being paid off, and retirement is in sight. It might feel like you have been given a raise and your saving muscle will strengthen again.

The key is to actually put savings aside when discretionary income is at its highest. Overcompensating during these years can help reduce stress in times where spending peaks.

[11]
What's Your Number?—Following Your Net Worth

For some of you, it might take less time to find Beyoncé's net worth number than your own. Fortunately for her, it's just an online search away. Unfortunately for most of us, our net worth isn't exactly "Internet worthy."

The key to financial success isn't what you make, but rather what you keep. So, if there is one number you should know, it's your net worth. Knowing this number keeps you motivated to continue saving. If you don't know your number, take a little time to tally what you own (assets), subtract what you owe (liabilities) and, voilà—meet your net worth.

The number itself doesn't matter as much as how it changes over time, so don't worry if it's negative right out of school or after buying your first house. A trend upward tells you that you're making progress by paying down debts, contributing more to savings and investment accounts, and/or your assets are appreciating in value. Revisit your number annually (or even more if you'd like) to see how much progress you've made. We can't promise it will get your number trending online, but it can help keep your priorities in line.

Two $ense

Common assets include house value, retirement accounts, other investment accounts, cars, and bank accounts. Common liabilities include home mortgages, student loans, credit card balances, home equity lines of credit, and car loans.

End of Chapter Resources

Personal Spending Worksheet
Net Worth Worksheet
Online Financial Calculator
Savings Rule of Thumb Video
The Power of Compounding Video

To access the end of chapter resources, go to
www.GetTheSense.com/Book-Resources.

Chapter 3

Everyday Money

Living, breathing, loving . . . sounds easy, but, in reality, doing life is a lot to ask. From raising children to maintaining a romantic relationship, throw in purchasing a car, buying a house, fulfilling philanthropic desires, and trying to keep your home in a somewhat organized state, one could jot down "Professional Juggler" as their true occupation. In this chapter, we hope to simplify some major life decisions, so that maybe, just maybe, there's room for a little vacationing in that busy schedule of yours . . . or maybe just a nap.

[12]

Vroom, Vroom—Buying a Car

New car smell, soft leather seats, shiny new paint, and, these days, a technological dream . . . the car-buying experience really is "sense"sational. Eyeing that new car can be like having a new crush—everything seems worth it, and it can be tempting to jump right in. Like any new relationship, it's important to think it through and not let your emotions get the best of you. So, before you drive off in your shiny new whip, consider these car-buying tips to help keep yourself—and your budget—together.

Do Some Recon: The Internet makes it easy to get the dirt on a new purchase. Educate yourself online before negotiating with a dealership or private party. Truecar.com is a great resource to see what the car of your dreams has been selling for in your local area.

Don't Be Needy: We recommend exploring financing through a bank or credit union prior to heading to the lot, as rates might be more competitive than at the dealer. It can also be quite amusing when the dealer agrees to come down on price, thinking he can increase your interest rate to make up for it. Show up toward the end of the day when salespeople and managers are eager to close the deal and get home. Waiting until the end of the month or quarter, when sales targets need to be met, can also give you negotiating leverage. Finally, consider buying from a local dealership. It might be more flexible on price with the hope that you will use their business to service your car in the future.

Consider Your Options: It's easy to get swept away by the newest model, but is it worth the price? You could pay as much as 30%–40% over the price of a three-year-old model. Granted, buying new comes with peace of mind about the condition of the car, plus a warranty from the manufacturer. However, there are tools, such as Carfax.com, available to help minimize the risk of buying a used car. Even better, many dealers offer Certified Pre-Owned cars that have undergone extensive screening and qualify for an extended warranty.

Define the Relationship: Although television ads make leasing appear incredibly inexpensive, it can have major drawbacks and can end up costing much more overall than buying a car outright. Leasing works best if you already plan to trade your car in every three to four years, if you don't want to hassle with maintenance costs, and if you drive less than the allowable mileage. A major downside to leasing is that you are forced to make a major financial decision every few years. Will you negotiate a new lease or buy the car? The more prudent financial decision is to skip the lease and drive your car for seven to ten years. If you are nearing the end of your lease, be sure to compare your residual value (buyout cost) to the market value of your car—it might be worth more than you pay (win).

Think beyond the Honeymoon Phase: Financing is usually not free. A $30,000 car might actually cost an extra $2,300 in interest. And, don't forget the additional financial commitments you might be making—especially if you are upgrading. You might need to consider increasing your auto insurance liability limits and comprehensive coverage. On top of traditional insurance, you might want to consider "gap" insurance, which will pay the difference between what you owe and what your car is worth, if it gets totaled. Gap insurance is often cheaper through your insurance company, so, when the dealer offers it—and he will—decline. When budgeting for a new car, consider the cost of upgrading over time. In addition to the cost of the car itself, other items might increase, such as insurance, registration, personal property tax, gas, repairs, maintenance, and even car washes.

Two $ense

Remember the registration you paid for on your old car? Consider it gone. You won't get a refund, even if you paid in November and sold/traded in your car in December. Consider this cost and perhaps time your new purchase closer to your registration renewal.

[13]
His, Hers, and Ours—Marriage and Finances

They say that the secret to a happy marriage is having separate bathrooms. We're not so sure that this private space is the key to marital bliss (or that realistic for most), but there is something to be said for keeping a few things separate in a marriage. Cash might be one of those things. Although there are many viable options, more couples are starting to take the "his, hers, and ours" approach to cash. Prefer shared bathrooms and checking accounts? That's great too. Whatever approach you choose, keep these tips in mind for a financially healthy marriage.

Consider sitting down with your spouse or partner to define shared goals and priorities. Touch base on your budget a couple times a year to make sure you are staying on track with your shared plan. Identify what portion of your take-home pay can be allocated toward discretionary spending. Although it might seem like every last dollar is used to cover "needs," the reality is that most of us spend 10%–30% of our pay on "wants" (for example, cable, dinners out, and entertainment). From this discretionary pool, agree on an amount that you can each spend as you please. This will provide both of you with the freedom to "do you" without feeling guilty or disrupting the family budget. Even better, it will allow for just enough secrecy to surprise (or be surprised!) with a great gift.

Finally, be open and honest (no hiding purchases in your car)! May your arguments be more about hogging the bathroom and less about money!

Two $ense

For traditional newlyweds, make sure to change your name with the U.S. Social Security Administration before filing your first tax return as a married couple. Your return cannot be processed if your name doesn't match that tied to your Social Security number. Also, because a new marriage means a new financial situation, review your payroll withholdings, and adjust on Form W-4, if needed (your financial advisor can help).

[14]
A Balancing Act—Buying a House

Life is one big balancing act of competing priorities. Just as you strive to find a balance with your time, it is also important to balance financial priorities. Buying a house is one of the largest purchases you will make, and it is one of the easiest ways to get out of financial balance. To understand your options, it is important to understand what a lender believes you can afford, but, before making your final decision, we encourage you to create your own definition of affordability.

To get an idea of the amount that a lender would be willing to extend, there are two key ratios to understand:

1. **Debt-to-Income Ratio (DTI):** Lenders typically require that all debt payments, including your potential mortgage payment, credit cards, car loans, child support, student loan debts and any other liability payments, be no more than 36% of your monthly gross (before-tax) income. This limit might vary from lender to lender and will likely be affected by other factors, such as your credit score and amount of your down payment. Some lenders will allow for as high as a 43% DTI ratio.

2. **Housing Ratio:** Specific to just the cost for housing, lenders prefer that your monthly housing payments, which include principal, interest, property tax, and insurance (PITI) and home owner association (HOA) dues (if applicable) do not surpass 28% of your monthly gross income.

Be careful before making a purchase decision based on a lender's definition of affordability. Be sure to check it against your own. Your definition of "afford" should not be based solely on cash flow but rather in light of your other goals, both now and in the future. To help put the size of your mortgage into some personal perspective, ask yourself the following questions:

- Will we be able to continue to save 20% of our after-tax income for retirement?

- Will our expenses increase in the future and can we fully cover them (for example, children, college, and care for aging parents)?

- Will we be able to comfortably spend on other financial priorities, like travel, private school, or personal care?

Despite what a lender might think, you might decide that allocating 28% of your income toward a new house is not practical. On the other hand, living in your dream home might be well worth it to you. After careful consideration, the decision is all yours!

Two $ense

Buying? The best time to buy a house is during the winter because fewer people are buying during the school year or the holidays. Renting? Note that the housing ratio is 30%, not 28%.

[15]
Lending an ARM and a Leg—Financing a House

When you are in the market to buy a house, your Realtor will suggest that you arrange your financing ahead of time, and a preapproval letter from your lender is often required when submitting an offer. Having a general understanding of financing options ahead of time can help you make one of  your biggest financial decisions a prudent one. Here is an overview of the most common mortgage types and considerations for each.

Fixed-Rate Mortgage (FRM): By far the most commonly used form of financing, the interest rate on a fixed-rate mortgage, and monthly payments, are fixed for the term of the loan—most often ten, fifteen, or thirty years. Payments are lower on thirty-year mortgages, because the repayment period is longer. However, interest rates are lower for shorter-term, ten- or fifteen-year loans. If cash flow is high, and you would like to pay off your mortgage faster or before a certain date, like retirement, a shorter term might make sense. If you prefer lower payments, consider a thirty-year mortgage instead. Fixed-rate mortgages are fiscally responsible, because set monthly payments are applied to interest and principal, steadily reducing your liability, and, therefore, increasing your net worth over time.

Adjustable-Rate Mortgage (ARM): Also commonly used for financing, interest rates on adjustable-rate mortgages are fixed only for a portion of the term (most often five or seven years), then the rate adjusts each year thereafter. The new rate is tied to an index rate, such as the *LIBOR rate*, plus additional percentage points, which will vary by lender. Once loan rates become variable and subject to annual adjustments, your payment will adjust to the amount required to *amortize* the balance of the loan at the current rate over the remaining loan term. The adjustable nature of rates and payments make ARMs riskier than fixed-rate options. ARM borrowers take a chance that they will move before the fixed-rate period ends, that income will increase in the future to support higher payments, or that interest rates will go down. Given the uncertainty of these variables, it is hard to make the case for an ARM for most borrowers looking to buy a house. ARMs might be better suited for real estate investors looking for *non-residence* purchases that they anticipate selling within the fixed term.

Interest-Only Mortgage: As the name implies, interest-only mortgages only require payments of interest and do not pay down principal. During the interest-only term, the balance of the liability does not decrease, and your net worth does not improve. Typically, interest-only loans are fixed interest for a period of seven or ten years, and then adjust to fully amortized, variable-rate loans requiring payments that include principal and interest for the balance of the loan term. Tackling principal on a now-shorter loan term (still continuing to pay interest) can dramatically increase payments. Similar to ARMs, interest-only borrowers make some predictions about the future, anticipating that they can pay off the loan balance or that they will sell the property before the interest-only term ends. The use of interest-only loans should be limited to speculators and experienced real estate investors. Remember that the housing ratio discussed in the previous entry includes principal payments. So, if you are just within the housing ratio but are basing housing costs on interest-only payments, the house is really more than you can responsibly afford.

In addition to financing options, your lender might also have a discussion with you about points. Mortgage points are fees paid up front, in exchange for a lower interest rate. One point will cost 1% of the planned loan balance. So, on a $500,000 mortgage, one point will cost $5,000. In exchange for paying points, your interest rate might drop by one-eighth (0.125%) to one-quarter (0.250%), on average. A lower interest rate for a long period of time can save a lot of money, but there are other factors to consider and break-even is important. Before deciding to pay points up front, divide your monthly savings (with the lower rate) by the cost of the point(s). If you do not plan to carry your mortgage for at least this long, an upfront cost might not be worth it. For this reason, many borrowers choose to add the cost of points to the loan balance to be paid down over time.

While we believe that there is a place for risk in your financial life, we don't believe that your primary or secondary house is the place for risk. For this reason, we favor fixed-rate mortgages. Also, because mortgage points vary by lender, work with your financial advisor to determine if paying points makes sense.

Two $ense

Before choosing a lender, be sure to get quotes from several lenders to find the best rate and lowest cost. Remember, it doesn't hurt to ask for a lower rate; your lender may surprise you.

[16]
Set, but Don't Forget—Refinancing a Mortgage

Your home is likely your largest asset and your mortgage your largest debt. Because payments typically stay the same, your mortgage is easy to set and forget. However, a small tweak to your largest liability can make a big difference to your cash flow and overall net worth. We urge you to review your mortgage every year or two to at least make sure it is still competitive in the current interest rate environment. If not, you might consider refinancing.

When does it make sense to refinance? If interest rates have decreased by 0.5% or more, then it might make financial sense (and be worth the time) to refinance. Use an online calculator to estimate what your new payment would be if you refinanced. Compare your new payment to your current payment to determine your potential savings. Keep in mind that refinancing isn't free, so it's important to weigh the costs of the refinance against the savings. To do so, divide the cost of the refinance by the amount you will save each month.

Let's use an example: Say that a refinance would save you $150 a month. If the cost to refinance is $2,000, it will take you a little more than thirteen months to "break-even" on your refi ($2,000/$150 = 13.33 months).

In general, if the break-even is fewer than twenty-four months, and you plan on staying in your home at least as long, then a refinance makes sense. Note that most lenders will require you to intend on living in the home for at least two years after a refinance to qualify for primary residence interest rates.

If you have had your mortgage for a long time, it might not make sense to refinance, even if rates have dropped substantially. To understand why, you need to understand how amortization works. In the beginning, most of a monthly payment is applied to satisfy interest on a loan, with a small portion applied toward principal. Over time, this trend reverses with more of the payment going toward paying down principal and less toward interest. With a new loan comes a new amortization schedule, again, with most of a payment going toward interest, effectively prolonging the payoff of principal. To visualize this, see the corresponding table.

Type:	Mortgage			Interest Rate:	4.500%
Payment Periods:	360			Payment Frequency:	Monthly

Year	Starting Balance	Payments	Interest	Principal Payments	Ending Balance
1	$250,000	($15,204)	$11,167	$4,037	$245,963
2	245,963	(15,204)	10,982	4,222	241,741
3	241,741	(15,204)	10,788	4,416	237,325
4	237,325	(15,204)	10,585	4,619	232,706
5	232,706	(15,204)	10,373	4,831	227,875
6	227,875	(15,204)	10,151	5,053	222,822
7	222,822	(15,204)	9,919	5,285	217,537
8	217,537	(15,204)	9,676	5,528	212,009
9	212,009	(15,204)	9,422	5,782	206,227
10	206,227	(15,204)	9,156	6,048	200,179

Year	Starting Balance	Payments	Interest	Principal Payments	Ending Balance
11	200,179	(15,204)	8,879	6,325	193,854
12	193,854	(15,204)	8,588	6,616	187,238
13	187,238	(15,204)	8,284	6,920	180,318
14	180,318	(15,204)	7,966	7,238	173,080
15	173,080	(15,204)	7,634	7,570	165,510
16	165,510	(15,204)	7,286	7,918	157,592
17	157,592	(15,204)	6,922	8,282	149,310
18	$149,310	($15,204)	$6,542	$8,662	$140,648
19	140,648	(15,204)	6,144	9,060	131,588
20	131,588	(15,204)	5,728	9,476	122,112
21	122,112	(15,204)	5,292	9,912	112,200
22	112,200	(15,204)	4,837	10,367	101,833
23	101,833	(15,204)	4,361	10,843	90,990
24	90,990	(15,204)	3,863	11,341	79,649
25	79,649	(15,204)	3,342	11,862	67,787
26	67,787	(15,204)	2,797	12,407	55,380
27	55,380	(15,204)	2,227	12,977	42,403
28	42,403	(15,204)	1,630	13,574	28,829
29	28,829	(15,204)	1,007	14,197	14,632
30	14,632	(14,987)	355	14,632	0

Two $ense

If you are nearing retirement, review your entire financial situation to see if a refinance makes sense. Refinancing might provide a way of tapping into your home equity while you still qualify, even if your mortgage is seasoned and interest is a small portion of your payment.

[17]
Consciously Uncouple—Divorce and Finances

Ugh. Divorce. Although it might seem like it, the world is not coming to an end—your world is just changing. One notion that becomes particularly important to understand when splitting assets in a divorce is that not every dollar is created equal. Depending on your situation, certain assets might be more valuable than others. When your "happily" turns out to be not so "ever after," consider the tips below to consciously uncouple your finances and to improve your financial health in the end:

Get Help: We don't mean from well-meaning friends and family. Seek the help of a professional. An hour of an attorney's time can pay off in spades, if he or she helps you negotiate a better settlement or identifies valuable alternatives. Consider this money well spent!

Find a Planner: To help ensure that you are looking at the big picture, consider working with a financial planner. A planner can provide referrals to, and play quarterback for, many key professionals you might want to consult, including a divorce attorney, CPA, an estate attorney, real estate agent, and mortgage broker. More important, a planner will help you plan for your new future.

Don't Take the House If You Can't Afford It: Especially when you have children, it is normal to want to minimize disruption to normal, everyday life. But, do not ask for the house if you can't afford it. Attempting to keep the status quo might not be the best long-term solution.

Consider Taxes: Certain retirement assets (for example, IRAs and 401(k)s) might be taxed as ordinary income when withdrawn, while others (for example, Roth IRAs and Roth 401(k)s) will not. All retirement plans have restrictions as to accessibility. If there are company-sponsored retirement plans to be split (for example, 401(k)s or pensions), familiarize yourself with the use of a *Qualified Domestic Relations Order (QDRO).* You might also pay tax on the sale of property or investments that have increased in value, so understand the after-tax value and sale costs of the assets before agreeing on the split.

Consider Taxes, Again: If you have children, understand what you could be giving up if you forgo the dependency exemption for tax filing. Head of Household filers pay income tax at a lower tax rate (compared to Single or Married filers), are eligible to claim a higher standard deduction, and might be able to take advantage of other tax credits, depending on income (for example, Dependent Care Credit or Earned Income Credit). It's well worth the money to have a CPA determine what you would be giving up in real dollars if you concede this status to your soon-to-be ex. This knowledge could save you thousands annually.

Plan for Debts: Consider an indemnity clause in the decree that will allow you to take action if your ex does not pay on a debt. Also, consider a refinancing clause for secured debts (for example, home or car) to remove your name from any liabilities, to be paid by your ex.

Protect Yourself: Just as important as protecting future income in a marriage, have the conversation about protecting child or spousal support payments in the event of death with the use of life insurance.

Two $ense

Know that alimony payments (spousal support) are taxable to the recipient and tax deductible by the payor. Child support, on the other hand, is tax-free to the recipient but not tax deductible by the payor.

Extra $ense

You owe it to yourself to stay involved in all transactions throughout your separation. For example, don't just sign your tax returns; protect yourself and review them with your CPA to understand the implications and monies owed or refunds due.

[18]
The More You Give, the More You Get—Philanthropy

We begin teaching our children from a young age that an important part of being good stewards of wealth is sharing with people or causes that are less fortunate. "Save, Spend, Share" jars are popular on Pinterest, because they help young savers visualize and form the habit of saving and giving. One way to get your kids involved is to sponsor a child their age in another country through a program that encourages an on-going pen pal-like relationship like Compassion International, World Vision, or Forever Changed International. As adults, we can lead by example by giving to the causes that are important to us.

Charitable giving is important primarily because it helps improve the lives of others, but there are also a few personal benefits. Despite popular belief, studies have shown that giving money to others improves donor happiness more than spending it on themselves. Additionally, it has been reported that the improved happiness and health of people who volunteer and make charitable contributions is likely linked to reduced rates of stress and lower blood pressure.

More than just psychological and physical benefits, there might also be income tax benefits associated with charitable donations. Donations to *501(c)(3)* charities result in an itemized deduction, which reduces taxable income for taxpayers who itemize. Most gifts to these qualified charities, except for the gift of time, qualify for a deduction. The most common gifts are cash or check, highly appreciated stock, or personal property (including clothes, furniture, books, etc.). Lesser-thought-of property that also makes a great charitable donation is real estate, cars, life insurance policies, and qualified direct distributions to charity from retirement plans.

For large charitable gifts, the amount of the deduction is limited to a percentage of your adjusted gross income (AGI), and varies based on the asset donated. For high-income earners, itemized deductions can be limited, however, the benefit of the charitable deduction will still help to reduce taxes. Charitable tax benefits are not available for taxpayers who take the standard deduction.

Even if you don't have highly appreciated stock or much cash to give, making simple gifts of time, clothes, or small recurring donations to your church or charity will still go a long way. We encourage you to enjoy the gift of giving by incorporating philanthropy into your life.

Two $ense

To make a charitable donation with a lasting impact, consider using a ***donor-advised fund (DAF)***. Donor-advised funds allow you to get a charitable tax deduction in the year you make the contribution, but allow you to make gifts to charities throughout your lifetime. From your DAF, you have the flexibility to set up auto payments to your church or any qualified charity, or simply make a gift once a year. You can also give the joy of giving to others by allowing them to direct a donation to a charity of their choice from your DAF. The minimum initial contribution to a DAF is usually about $5,000 and can be invested, so a little can go a long way.

End of Chapter Resources

Your Financial Life after Divorce Checklist

To access the end of chapter resources, go to
www.GetTheSense.com/Book-Resources.

Chapter 4

The Kiddos

Parents are likely to list the birth of their first child as one of the most pivotal days of their lives. Priorities change when someone else's life is completely dependent on you. Most new parents have appropriate expectations that their personal lives will change (goodbye sleeping in, brunch, and late nights out; hello playdates, stroller joggers, and story time), yet few parents are prepared for the financial impact that comes with having a child—it's more than the cost of diapers, baby food, and clothing. Here, we'll give you our best thoughts on the major money issues directly related to your little and not-so-little ones.

[19]
Decisions, Decisions—Planning for Childcare

Name, hospital, nursery colors, delivery method, vaccinations, vitamins, cord banking, siblings . . . The list of decisions when having a baby is endless. It's no wonder people say you'll never be fully ready! Of the many possible decisions, perhaps one of the most financially significant is whether one parent will stay home (on a full-or part-time basis) and what type of child care will make the most sense. This is a personal decision and not one that we would try to make for you. Instead, because the cost of child care is a primary factor for many parents-to-be, we want to provide a roundup of the three most common options and related costs for your consideration.

Nanny: $17–$20 per hour (at least $680 weekly or $35,360 annually, if full-time). If you prefer to have your child stay at home for care, consider hiring a nanny. A trusted friend might provide a recommendation, or agencies such as <u>Care.com</u>, <u>4nannies.com</u>, <u>Enannysource.com</u> can also do a great job of running background checks, checking past experience, and obtaining referrals. Interview multiple candidates and trust your instincts.

Mom Tip: If you hire a nanny, randomly check in and don't be afraid to consider a nanny cam. It's your child and your rules.

Day Care: $9–$11 per hour (at least $360 weekly or $18,720 annually, if full-time). Day care is typically less expensive than a nanny and might provide for a more structured environment of established school routines, reliable hours (no need to take off work for a sick nanny), and more public monitoring of care. Many parents also like exposing their child to group learning activities and a more social environment.

Mom Tip: Look for a day care close to home or work, even if it costs a bit more. Convenience and family time are priceless.

Au Pair: $8–$10 per hour (at least $320 weekly or $16,640 annually, if full-time). An au pair is a domestic assistant from a foreign country working for, and living as part of, a host family. The key takeaway here is "live-in." Typically, au pairs take on a share of the family's responsibility for child care along with some housework in exchange for a monetary allowance. An au pair tends to be the most flexible of child care options and can work well for parents with unpredictable schedules. Of course, you'll need to be open to an added roommate and have an extra room for privacy. You can get more information at sites such as Culturalcareaupair.com or Aupaircare.com.

Mom Tip: If you expect that your au pair will be driving your car, be sure to add him or her as an insured driver on your auto policy.

Two $ense

When comparing child care costs to the opportunity cost of staying home, remember to consider after-tax income, the value of employee benefits (for example, 401(k) match or health insurance), and future earning potential that might be reduced or lost if you decide to stay home or work less.

[20]

Put Your Mask On—Prioritizing College Savings and Costs

"In the event of the loss of cabin pressure, an oxygen mask will automatically appear in front of you. Pull the mask toward you and place it firmly over your nose and mouth, securing the elastic band behind your head, and breathe normally. If you are traveling with a child or someone who requires assistance, secure your mask first, and then assist the other person."

—Flight Attendant Safety Briefing

This familiar preflight warning is necessary because the instinct to help others—especially our children—is so strong that we might be inclined to assist them before helping ourselves. While not as dramatic as a loss of cabin pressure, the urge to help children get through college is so strong that many well-intentioned parents stop or reduce saving for retirement in exchange for their children's education. If you expect that retirement and college will be competing financial priorities (and you're not alone), we encourage you to secure your retirement mask first, so that helping your children now doesn't mean leaning on them for assistance later.

The annual cost of a four-year public college in 2017 is $24,610 and for a private institution it is $49,329 (in-state tuition assumed). That's tough, even today, if you have an 18 year-old, but if your child is a newborn and costs inflate by 5% a year, the total cost could be $200,000 for public school and $400,000 for private! So, how much should you be saving? Assuming a 6% rate of return, if you plan to fully fund college:

Estimated Monthly Savings to Pay 100% of College Costs		
Age of Child	Public, Four-Year	Private, Four-Year
0	$552/mo.	$1,106/mo.
5	$677/mo.	$1,357/mo.
10	$914/mo.	$1,833/mo.

Even on a monthly basis, these numbers can be scary, particularly when you have other goals (for example, not working forever). Consider saving to a *529 college savings plan* (a tax-advantaged savings plan) to help make this goal more attainable, and keep in mind that many families do not expect to cover 100% of college costs. Work with your financial advisor to determine how much you can afford to cover, while still saving for retirement, or use Savingforcollege.com's calculator to develop your ideal savings target. If fully funding college and reaching your retirement goal are out of reach, here are some alternatives to consider:

Pay for Part: Pay what you can afford while saving for other goals. Consider ways to cover the balance, like having your child take out student loans or work during breaks and during the school year.

Be a Scholarship Sleuth: There are plenty of scholarships available, and the small ones can really add up. Know that your child will lose out on 100% of the scholarship opportunities for which he or she does not apply.

Be a Smart Consumer: At some point, the marginal value of attending one school over another wanes. Consider the value of in-state colleges, which cost less to attend, living at home, and whether your child's dream school has a practice of accepting transfer students from less-expensive community or junior colleges.

Think of the college discussion as an opportunity to communicate valuable financial lessons to your children. Help them understand the financial sacrifices that were made to give them an education. Perhaps you decided to work two more years or gave up buying a new car, second home, or going on vacation. Perspective can create gratitude and set expectations.

Regardless of how much you contribute, plan ahead and communicate. You both might breathe just a bit easier.

[21]
Numbers of the Day—529 College Savings Plans

Baby Einstein, Disney Junior, Nickelodeon . . . education stays top of mind at every age. Just as learning should start early, so should saving for education, regardless of how much you can afford to save. As you sing along with Sesame Street's daily number ditties, we encourage you to remember three important digits: 5, 2, and 9, as 529 plans are one of the most tax-efficient ways to save for college. Although there are other saving options available, here are the top three reasons to consider 529 plans:

Less Tax Means More for College: Investment earnings in a 529 plan grow tax-deferred, and distributions used to pay for qualified higher education expenses might be taken tax-free. Sheltering investment tax on growth allows for more money to stay invested, compounding growth faster. Although contributions to 529 plans are not federally tax deductible, some states allow contributions by residents to be deductible at the state level.

Flexibility: To maximize 529 plan benefits, funds really should be used for college, but flexibility is far from lost. For starters, compared to other savings vehicles that allow children to take full control of assets as early as age 18, 529 funds allow parents to maintain control of plan assets, indefinitely. Additionally, although each account is set up with just one beneficial child, funds don't need to be used for that child. In the event one child doesn't go to college or use all his or her funds, plan assets can be used to fund college for other siblings or family members, simply by changing the beneficiary. Finally, taxes will apply, but in the event of a financial hardship, plan assets are always available (earnings are subject to a 10% penalty plus ordinary income tax).

A Simple and Group Effort: 529 accounts can be opened online, and, once established, loved ones can easily contribute. Birthday and holiday gifts from family members and friends can really add up. With competing financial priorities, like home ownership and retirement, making college savings a group effort might be necessary. Annual $50 birthday gifts from just four family members can add up to more than $6,000 over time, which will go a lot further than a disposable toy!

Two $ense

While 529 plans do not have annual contribution limits, funds added to these plans are considered *gifts* and might have gift tax implications. In 2017, the IRS allows an individual to gift up to $14,000 in cash or property to as many people as he or she desires, without triggering any gift tax consequences. Some exceptions apply but, in general, gifts in excess of $14,000 must be reported on a gift tax return. This does not mean that the gifts will be subject to taxation. A gift tax return is simply a way of keeping track of annual gifts made in excess of the allowable amount. Only until this tally exceeds the lifetime exclusion amount of $5.49 million (in 2017) will gifts in excess of $14,000 be subject to gift tax (and the responsibility of the giver, not the receiver). The 529 plan has a unique exception to these gifting rules in that a lump sum equal to five years of annual gifting can be contributed without chipping away at the lifetime exclusion amount. For example, in 2017, a married couple can contribute up to $140,000 ($14,000 each x 5) to a child's 529 plan, but must not make any additional contributions for the next five years.

[22]
Training Wheels . . . Again—Teaching Good Money Habits

Mood swings, voice changes, acne, OPINIONS . . . these are all signs that your baby is growing up. While we can't tell you how to deal with the joys of puberty, we can help you with the financial transition of teenage independence. At some point, you might begin to consider plastic as an alternative to sending your teen off with wads of cash. Worried that he or she will overspend or mess up your credit? We don't blame you. So, instead of a credit card, consider a debit card as your teen's first plastic—a credit card with training wheels. While a debit card won't build your teen's credit, it will still provide benefits for both of you.

Controlled Convenience: Give your teen the convenience of a credit card without going into debt or messing up anyone's (*ahem,* your) credit. Help control spending and opt out of any overdraft protection options to limit purchases to just the account balance. Also, consider limiting the amount of a single draw to a few hundred dollars.

Security: Losing a debit card will provide more protection than losing cash. Know that fraud protection varies by issuer—some credit card company–sponsored debit cards provide just what is available under Federal law and others provide more. Federal law will cap the loss to $50 if your teen notifies the bank within two days of learning of the theft. But, if your teen procrastinates a few days, the cap might jump to $500, and he or she could lose everything if they wait too long (60+ calendar days). And, because teens have been known to withhold information, encourage them to tell you the minute their card might be lost. We recommend text transaction alerts, which can help you keep an eye on your teen's spending and potential fraud.

Practice: Setting spending parameters with a debit card can teach your teen not to spend more than he or she can pay off each month. This will be their single most important money habit before applying for their first credit card as an adult. A little practice can make for a better-than-average spender.

If you think your teen is ready to ditch the training wheels, you can help him or her start establishing credit by adding them as an authorized user on your credit card. However, remember that their charges are your charges, and their lost credit card is your lost credit card!

Two $ense

Be sure not to confuse a prepaid card with a debit card. Unless they are sponsored by companies providing special fraud coverage, prepaid cards don't carry the same minimum Federal protections as a debit card against loss or disputed charges.

[23]
Outside the Gift Box—Financially Savvy Gifts

If you asked your children what their top five favorite birthday presents were, what do you think they'd say? Maybe it was their Barbie jeep, the spring break airline tickets, the puppy you surprised them with, or their first car. We feel fairly safe in making the assumption that the gifts our children usually remember are the bigger-ticket items or the ones that provide a longer-lasting experience. So, we asked ourselves, "What kind of gift can we get our loved ones that could have an ever-lasting impact and be a present that is literally unforgettable?" Stick with us on this concept for a moment longer . . .

We've come up with a few unconventional gift ideas that can leave *both* a financial and everlasting memorable impact. For those looking to mix things up, we encourage you to add these to your gift-giving repertoire:

Give the Gift of Compounding. If the youth in your life are earning a paycheck, then they're eligible to save in a Roth IRA. The likelihood of them doing this on their own is probably close to that of a democracy in North Korea. So, be the superhero mom or auntie and make a contribution on their behalf. The money seed you plant today will grow alongside the recipient and be a continual gift that keeps on giving.

Deck the Dorm Halls. Get started growing tax-free savings for college expenses by opening a 529 plan. Tell everyone you know (better yet, keep it to those who actually like your kids), that little Henry could use a token toy to open and a check for his future. Consider it to be your friends and family college discount! Another idea, cover the cost of a semester of course books—supporting higher education for your loved ones is surely not a sunk cost.

Stuff Their Stocking. Put the "stock" in stocking . . . literally. Make someone a part owner in a company that they love. Physical shares of stock can be purchased online through websites such as Giveashare.com. If the site doesn't have what you're looking for, consider buying (or giving your own shares) through your brokerage firm.

Spread the Wealth. Ask your loved ones how they would best like to make a difference in the world and make a donation to a charity in their name. Amazon Smile has made it easier than ever by providing the option to donate a portion of qualified purchases to a charity (or charities) of your choice, with the same conveniences as Amazon Prime.

Need ideas? Browse a broad range of charities through independent vetting websites, like GuideStar.org or GiveWell.org, or, if you're specifically interested in military charities, check out ThePatriotsInitiative.org.

If you're throwing a birthday party—or really, any party—give your child the option to forgo presents and instead sponsor a charity, cause, or child that guests can make a donation toward. Utilize this as an educational opportunity with your child to discuss the concepts of giving back, counting his or her blessings for what they have, and sharing in the warm and fuzzy feeling one gets when helping others.

End of Chapter Resources

Gifting the Wealthy Way

To access the end of chapter resources, go to
www.GetTheSense.com/Book-Resources.

Chapter 5

Retirement

From Social Security and income planning to Medicare and long-term care, there are enough retirement concepts to fill a book—and there are a lot of books. While retirement guides can be helpful, they tend to be general. We believe that your plan for riding off into the retirement sunset should be anything but general. If retirement is a near-term goal, work with a financial advisor to create your own, unique retirement plan. Our goal for this chapter is to help those with a longer timeframe maximize and prioritize retirement savings.

[24]
Image Isn't Everything—Savings Checkpoints

In a world dominated by social media, it's important to remember that image isn't everything. Apps like Instagram and Facebook make it easy for users to portray carefully crafted brands—personal marks that might or might not be an accurate reflection of reality. Comparing your life to the calculated, perfectly filtered images of another can create feelings of insecurity or fear of missing out (FOMO).

If your newsfeed, full of world travels, flashy new cars, designer handbags, and new houses, has you feeling financially inadequate, we'd like to point out that no one ever posts their checking account balances, 401(k) contributions, or credit card statements. Instant gratification might come with a cost of working forever. If you would like to retire someday, instead of comparing your financial health to misleading overshares, use our simple, black-and-white, emoji and filter-free chart to see if you're savings are on track.

Tally up the amounts in your savings account, retirement plans, IRAs, and anywhere else you might be stashing money away to see if you are on course.

Retirement Savings by Age Checkpoints	
Age	Savings Target (multiply this number by your current before-tax income)
30	1x
35	2x
40	3x
45	4x
50	6x
55	7x
60	8x
65	9x
70	10x

Two $ense

Think you can't afford to save? Remember this: A dollar saved to your employer's 401(k) or other retirement plan will not feel like a dollar lost from your paycheck. Earnings that are not directed to these plans will be subject to federal and state income tax withholding, so a dollar earned will only give you about sixty cents to spend anyway. But, saving on a pre-tax basis to these plans means that you get to invest every penny for yourself! How can you afford not to?

[25]
Pyramid of Success—Savings Hierarchy

You have some money to set aside, but what are you going to do with it? You're not alone in not knowing how to put your money to work. It is so common an inquiry, in fact, that just searching "where should I put . . . ?" prompts an eerily clairvoyant online search to know that you probably want to ask where to put your money (immediately followed by where to put your subwoofer, but we can't help you with that).

Most savers are probably looking for investment help, but what you should really determine first is, (1) if you are in a financial position to be investing, and (2) if so, the type of account in which you should invest.

The number-one priority for extra cash is paying off bad debts (for example, credit card debt), followed by establishing an adequate emergency fund, and then saving for retirement. Where to save for retirement might be confusing, given the number of factors to consider (account types, tax implications, employer contributions, etc.). If you are prepared to begin saving for retirement, the corresponding pyramid provides the generally accepted order for where to put your next saved dollar.

**Account Type
(In Order of Priority)**

Employer plan [401(k), Roth 401(k), 403(b), 457]
Contribution Amount: Amount needed to receive
maximum employer match ("free money")

Then . . .

Roth IRA
2017 Maximum Contribution: $5,500
2017 catch-up (age 50+): $1,000
Income might affect eligibility

Then back to . . .

**Employer plan [401(k), Roth 401(k),
403(b), 457]**
Contribution Amount: Maximum
amount allowed by the IRS
2017 maximum contribution: $18,000
2017 catch-up (age 50+): $6,000

Then . . .

Traditional IRA
2017 Maximum
Contribution: $5,500
2017 catch-up
(age 50+): $1,000
Income might affect
deductibility

Then . . .

Nonretirement Account
Contribution Amount:
Unlimited contributions

Two $ense

Your company match is just that—a match. If your contributions from each paycheck reach the annual IRS limit before the end of the year, your employer might stop your paycheck contributions. And, you guessed it . . . no contributions by you could mean no match by your employer, and income earned for the balance of the year could go unmatched. If you expect to max out in a year, contribute a set dollar amount from each paycheck versus a percentage of your pay to ensure that you don't max out early and miss out. Check with your Human Resources department to see if your employer offers a "true-up" contribution at the end of the year to fix this common oversight.

[26]
Not Just a Name—IRA Accounts

You might be surprised to learn that "Ira" is not one of the most popular baby names. Yeah . . . we weren't either. But, these three little letters, when capitalized, should become much more attractive to you and your future: IRA.

What is an IRA? An IRA is an Individual Retirement Arrangement that allows you to save for retirement and receive tax advantages. As long as you are under the age of 70½, and you or your spouse have earned income, you can save to an IRA. There are two types of IRAs, and the major tax perk of both is tax-deferral. Unlike a regular investment account, there will be no income tax liability on the earnings generated by the investments in an IRA, which means your savings can compound faster. In exchange for these tax advantages, IRA funds cannot be withdrawn without a penalty tax before the age of 59½. So, if you are saving for a new car, college, or anything else that you will want before age 59½, an IRA would not be your vehicle of choice.

What are the types of IRAs? The two types of IRAs are traditional and Roth. While the tax-deferral feature is the same for both, contributions and withdrawals are treated differently.

Traditional IRA: If eligible, you might receive an income tax deduction for contributions (taxable income is reduced by amount contributed). The tradeoff for this up-front tax deduction is that every dollar withdrawn will be taxed as ordinary income. Unfortunately, you won't be able to kick the tax can down the road forever. The IRS requires a minimum amount be withdrawn and taxed each year, beginning at age 70½.

Roth IRA: If you are eligible to contribute to a Roth IRA, you will not receive an income tax deduction for contributions. The upside is that contributions can be withdrawn tax-free at any time and distributions of earnings might also be tax-free. To take tax-free distributions of earnings, you must be at least 59½ *and* your initial contribution must have been made at least five years prior to the date of the distribution. There are no minimum distribution requirements at age 70½ (can kicked)!

What's All This "If You Are Eligible" Talk? Although you may always contribute to a traditional IRA—provided you are less than age 70½, and you or your spouse have earned income—you might not receive a tax deduction for the full contribution amount. Also, your income might affect your eligibility to contribute to a Roth IRA all together. Learn the rules of the game in the next entry.

Two $ense

Alimony received counts as earned income for purposes of making IRA contributions. According to the IRS, you've earned every penny of it!

[27]
Rules of the Game—IRA Contributions

There are rules to the game of saving for retirement, specifically certain eligibility considerations when contributing to IRAs. Understanding these eligibility rules helps identify your options when saving for retirement.

How much can I contribute? The maximum IRA contribution limit for 2017 is $5,500 ($6,500 if age 50+). Your total IRA contributions for the year—to traditional, Roth, or a combination of both—cannot exceed these limits. Also, contributions cannot exceed your income for the year. For example, a college student with $4,000 in wages may only make a $4,000 contribution. If you contribute more than what is allowed in a year and fail to take corrective action, there will be a 6% penalty tax for every year the excess amount remains in the IRA.

Traditional IRA

Deductibility: The tax deduction you receive for contributing to an IRA might be reduced based on two factors: retirement plans through work and your *Modified Adjusted Gross Income (MAGI)*. If you or your spouse is an active participant[1] in a workplace retirement plan and your MAGI exceeds the annual threshold, you can still fund a traditional IRA, but your deductibility will be affected. It's important to point out that being a high-income earner will not prevent you from taking the deduction, if neither you or your spouse are active participants. Don't let your decision to contribute hinge on deductibility alone, because your contributions to an IRA will still grow tax-deferred, which is a powerful thing.

Roth IRA

Contributions: Unlike a traditional IRA to which you can always make contributions, Roth IRA contributions might be reduced or disallowed all together if your MAGI exceeds the annual limit. MAGI is the only factor that determines Roth IRA contribution eligibility (active participant rules do not apply).

---

1   An individual is considered an active participant if he/she participates in or receives contributions (including company contributions or forfeitures) to an employer-sponsored defined benefit plan, money purchase plan, profit-sharing plan, 401(k) plan, 403(a) or 403(b) plan, SEP IRA and/or SIMPLE IRA, or a plan established by any governmental agency.

Two $ense

Non-deductible traditional IRA contributions are reported on IRS Form 8606. This is an important form to keep because it serves as proof that these contributions should not be subject to tax when later withdrawn.

Extra $ense

Since Roth IRA contributions are not tax-deductible, they are not reported on tax returns. To keep track of your contributions, keep a copy of Form 1099-R with your tax return documents. Form 1099-R provides a record for your contribution and will be provided by your account custodian in every year that a contribution is made.

[28]
Worth the Wait—Traditional vs. Roth

Instant gratification has become a cultural norm, but some things are just worth waiting for. Black Friday, encores, and pumpkin spice lattes might come to mind. In the same way, delaying certain financial benefits can provide greater satisfaction in the long run. For those of you (and/or your spouse) who are offered a traditional and Roth 401(k) option through work, or are considering an IRA contribution, the decision on which type to fund essentially comes down to whether you want an income tax benefit now or later. Specifically, does it make more sense to receive a tax deduction this year or tax-free income later? A quick summary of tax benefits and timing for each plan type follows.

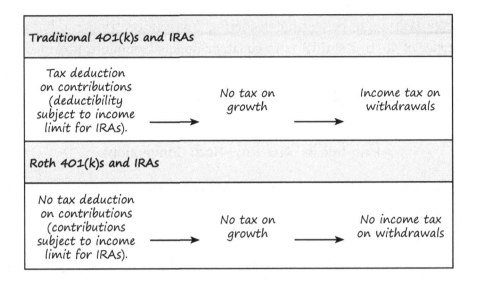

How to choose? If you are in your prime working years and your tax bracket is higher now than it will be when you expect to withdraw the funds in retirement, then it likely makes more sense to take advantage of the current-year tax deduction you would get by contributing to a traditional 401(k) or IRA. If, on the other hand, you believe that your tax bracket is lower now than it will be when you plan to withdraw funds, then you might be better off funding a Roth 401(k) or Roth IRA.

It's also important to consider the value of an income tax deduction throughout your working years. Deductions become more valuable as your income goes up. If you are just starting out and believe your income is lower than what it will be in later years (insert prayer emoji here), then the deduction might be more valuable in the future. So, it might make sense to forgo the income tax deduction now with Roth contributions and switch to a traditional 401(k) in peak earning years. If you are somewhere between, a combination approach might be worth considering. You can contribute to both types of 401(k)s and IRAs in equal, or unequal amounts, provided your total contributions do not exceed the maximum limit.

[29]
Pay Tax to Save Tax—Roth Conversions

The nature of a "tax benefit" is to pay less tax. In addition to making IRA contributions, there might be another tax-saving strategy with IRAs worth exploring: a Roth conversion.

A Roth conversion is the process of transferring (converting) all or part of the investments in your traditional IRA to a Roth IRA. Generally, any amount converted will be subject to income tax. Yes, we said it—pay tax—but, the goal is to pay tax now, so that you don't have to pay (potentially more tax) later.

A Roth conversion makes the most sense if, (1) you believe you will be in a lower tax bracket now than in the future, or you believe tax rates will increase; (2) you have sufficient funds outside of your IRAs to pay the income tax due; and (3) the conversion amount doesn't bump you into a higher tax bracket. Conversion can be worthwhile, but, as is the case with all things tax related, the devil is in the details. Work with a CPA to see if a conversion strategy makes sense for you.

[30]
Looks Good on Paper—Retirement Plan Investing

Let's face it, in the world of dating sites and apps, appearance matters. First impressions are formed on a handful of photos and limited character count, but anyone who has spent time in the online dating scene knows that the pictures painted by potential suitors do not tell the whole story.

Choosing investments in your 401(k) or other company plan is a lot like online dating. You are provided with a list of names from which to choose, a bit about their heritage (domestic or international, stocks or bonds) and some information about their past (performance). Just like with dating, you don't want to rely on an online profile to make this important decision. Ask the following "get to know you" questions about your options before making your selections.

What's on the inside? *Mutual fund* names tell you little about how they are actually invested. Review the fund's prospectus to learn more about its make-up or ask your financial advisor to take a look for you. If you aren't familiar with the "insides," you could be missing out on opportunities or doubling up on similar funds, potentially providing inadequate diversification.

Will it get along with others? Chemistry is important in a partner, but he or she also needs to fare well with other people in your life. The same goes for your investments. For example, if you and your spouse both have retirement plans or investments outside your company plans, it's important to make sure they all work well together. Perhaps your husband's plan offers the best small-cap stock fund and yours has a great large-cap stock fund. Rather than buying sub-par investments in both plans, allocate across plans to invest in only the best fund options.

Should I keep my options open? Although the goal for dating is to find "the one," the goal for investments is to diversify risk through multiple partners. How many investments you choose, and what type, all depends on your target *asset allocation*. Where you choose to hold the investments will depend on account types and fund options available.

Will I feel safe? Depending on your tolerance for risk, racecar driving might be a relationship deal breaker. Risk should also be considered when selecting investments. Do not just rely on performance provided online. The fund with the highest return might also be the one with more ups and downs than you can stomach. Ask your financial advisor to review risk measures, like *standard deviation* and *Sharpe ratio* to see if you will feel safe in the relationship.

[31]
Should I Stay or Should I Go?—Retirement Plan Options

Let's face it, the days of receiving a gold watch for thirty-plus years of service to one company is so 1980. We are living in a "move-on-to-move-up" culture and many of us have, or will, leave a trail of retirement plans in our wake. If you left your 401(k), 403(b), or other employer retirement plan behind because you've been busy and/or didn't know your options, this entry is for you. We have summarized your options and key considerations to help you weigh them. Note that there will be no tax implications for the options provided here.

Retirement Plan Options . . .	And Considerations
Roll Over to an IRA Once you leave your company (and in some cases, even before that), you have the option to roll your plan funds to an IRA.	Make an informed decision by comparing each of these important considerations with the help of a financial advisor:
Leave It Your old employer might allow you to leave your funds just where they are until you are ready to begin taking distributions. If you leave your employer between the ages of 55–59½, you can avoid tax penalties (10% federal plus a state penalty in some states) if you withdraw funds. This option is not available with an IRA.	**Fees** Employers might pass along some of the administrative costs of the plan to you as a participant and each investment option available has underlying expenses (known as expense ratios). An additional fee might also be charged if your plan provides for professional management. Compare all fees between your old plan, new plan, and IRA options and assess the value of these fees. For example, if the expense ratios in Plan A are higher than Plan B, but Plan B has better investment performance (after fees), it might be worth the move to Plan B. Similarly, an IRA through an advisor might offer broader financial planning services that are worth an extra expense.
Roll into a New Company Plan Your current employer will likely allow you to roll funds into your new plan. Consolidating accounts can help simplify the management of your retirement investments and your new plan might allow you to borrow funds in a pinch. Borrowing funds is not available with an IRA.	**Performance and Risk** Evaluate your investment options on the basis of performance (after-fees) and risk. Do not blindly accept the best performer as the ideal option as the amount of risk in the fund might be outside your level of comfort in future years. Also, be sure to compare like investments. For example, compare a large-cap growth stock fund in Plan A to a large-cap growth stock fund in Plan B or an IRA.

Retirement Plan Options . . .	And Considerations
	Flexibility Many employer plans have a limited number of investment options when compared to an IRA. Still, a comparison of fees, risk, performance, and services provided should be done before deciding that more is more with an IRA.
	Protection Most employer-plan types afford greater protection from creditors and lawsuits than when compared to an IRA. Depending on your circumstances, this additional protection might or might not make the case for keeping your funds in an employer plan.

Two $ense

One of the most common money mistakes is cashing out a retirement plan when leaving an employer. It is a tempting but costly option. Distributions will be taxed as ordinary income and, if under age 55, additional penalty taxes might apply. Plus, cashing out a $5,000 retirement plan could cost more than $15,000 in lost earnings during a thirty-year timeframe. Save on taxes and keep the funds invested in your new company plan or rollover IRA, instead.

[32]
The Hustle Is Real—Self-Employed Retirement Plan Options

Being an entrepreneur can be as difficult as spelling entrepreneur. Apart from the financial risk involved, there are a lot of decisions to be made when starting your own business, including product offering, marketing strategy, entity type, compensation arrangements, and other factors. Plus, unless you plan to work forever, you'll need to decide on a retirement plan. Choosing a retirement plan is one area that self-starting entrepreneurs might not want to go at alone; it will be complicated and can get more complicated if you have employees. To avoid costly mistakes and liability, we recommend working with a professional. Here, we will provide a foundation for the discussion that you should have with your advisor.

Popular small business retirement plans include SEP IRAs, SIMPLE IRAs, Solo 401(k)s, traditional 401(k)s, and defined benefit plans. The optimal plan will depend on a number of factors, including the amount and stability of extra cash flow that can be used to contribute to the plan and to maintain the plan (both now and in the future), your age, the age of your employees, employee turnover, and your general disposition toward generosity (certain plans require you to save on behalf of your employees, while others do not.)

In 2017, the maximum contribution limit for SEP IRAs, Solo 401(k)s, and traditional 401(k)s is $54,000, which might be reduced based on income and includes contributions made by the employer and the employee, where applicable. Defined benefit plan contributions might be much higher. Unlike SEP IRAs and 401(k)s, defined benefit plans do not have a contribution limit. Instead, they have a maximum *benefit* amount. Contributions can be made up to an amount that is expected to provide the maximum allowable benefit of $215,000 in retirement (2017). Professional actuaries determine required annual funding amounts for defined benefit plans. (We told you it would be complicated.)

Know that establishing certain retirement plans can be as simple as filling out an adoption agreement and completing an application through your brokerage firm. Although it's easy, you might find that your brokerage company is not fully equipped to help with plan-related questions or requests that might arise down the road. Instead, we recommend hiring a third-party administrator (TPA) to help with choosing a plan, drafting the plan document, preparing necessary tax filings, and managing plan requests, such as loans, rollovers, and distributions. It will be money well spent.

Popular Retirement Plan Highlights for Business Owners				
	SEP IRA	Simple IRA	Solo 401(k)	Defined Benefit
Contributions	Maximum contribution is 25% of net income (20% for Sole Proprietor) up to $54,000 (2017). Contributions are made solely by the employer, but are not required. If contributions are made, employees must receive the same contribution percentage as owners.	Maximum contribution $12,500, plus $3,000 catch-up age 50+ (2017) Contributions are made by employee salary deferrals and employer must make either a matching contribution up to 3% of compensation or contribute 2% of compensation (regardless of employee contributions).	Maximum contribution 25% of compensation or net income (20% for Sole Proprietor) or $54,000 (2017) Contributions may be made by owner as employer and as employee (salary deferrals).	Maximum contribution determined by an actuary; up to an annual benefit of $215,000 (2017) Contributions are solely employer paid and are generally required annually as set by plan terms.

Popular Retirement Plan Highlights for Business Owners				
	SEP IRA	Simple IRA	Solo 401(k)	Defined Benefit
Other Factors	Considered for businesses with variable income and without employees, unless employer wishes to equally contribute on behalf of employees.	Not available to employer with over 100 employees. Considered for businesses with or without employees that don't have an excess of cash flow.	Available only to owner plus spouse (no employees). Considered for businesses with higher free cash flow.	Employer must contribute amount needed to satisfy minimum funding requirement. Considered for businesses who desire to contribute more than amounts allowed by other plans and have high amounts of stable cash flow.

Chapter 6

Going Pro

If it hasn't happened already, there will likely come a point in your life when you decide to seek the guidance of a professional for either investment help, financial planning, or both. Unlike when hiring a professional to do your hair or to design your landscape project—services of which we don't feel the need to know anything about—there is a retained sense of responsibility when it comes to hiring someone to help with money. We often hear from our clients, "I should really know more, but I don't." We recommend finding a knowledgeable advisor that you trust, allowing you to focus on what you do best to provide for you and your family. Yet, there are a few basic concepts and considerations that we believe you should know to prepare you for working with a professional, and you'll find them in this chapter.

[33]
Thigh Bone's Connected to the Hip Bone—
Working with a Financial Advisor

You've finally found an hour in your day to get that annoying knot in your back worked on. So, why is your masseuse working on your legs and suggesting that you stretch your hamstrings? It's because all our muscles are connected and a kink in one is likely due to another. You might have a similar experience when you begin working with a financial advisor. You go in for assistance with one goal and come out with a list of seemingly unrelated things to address to reach that goal. You probably know when you need a massage (like, yesterday), but you might not know when you need a financial advisor (also probably yesterday).

What is a financial advisor? A financial advisor is a professional who helps individuals manage their finances by providing advice on money issues, such as budgeting, investments, insurance, debt, college savings, estate planning, taxes, retirement planning, etc.

Who needs a financial advisor? Every adult! No matter how much money you have, there are financial aspects of your life that will benefit from the help of a financial advisor. At a young age, the initial conversations will likely be centered on starting an emergency fund, investing in your company's 401(k), and taking advantage of compounding growth. As you get older, the conversations will shift to insurance needs, saving for college, and retirement planning.

How Do I Choose? Before searching for an advisor, know your personal deal breakers. What do you want, need, or expect from this professional? Then, start by asking friends and family for recommendations. Peruse the advisor's website to scope out the services he or she offers, get a feel for the approach and go in for a meeting to see if the advisor is a good fit (the first visit should be complimentary). In your initial meeting, we recommend asking a few key questions:

✓ What services do you provide? Investment advice, financial and retirement planning, insurance, others?

✓ Does your regulatory body hold you and your firm to the **Fiduciary Standard of Care?**

✓ What can I expect to pay in fees and/or commissions?

✓ What reputable third-party **custodian(s)** do you use for accounts?

Just as a total body approach to a massage is more effective, so is a comprehensive approach to your money. Your thigh bone is connected to your hip bone, and your tax bracket is directly connected to your retirement plan.

[34]
Management Fees for $100—Advisory Fees

Jeopardy contestants are challenged with delivering the precise question to an answer that is provided. If you work with a financial advisor, one of the most important questions you must ask relates to how much you are paying. After all, fees do chip away at your investment return. Here, semantics can play a big part in the answer that you are provided. To get the answer you are really looking for, you must *ask the right question* . . .

If you have hired a professional to choose investments on your behalf, you are likely paying a "management fee." This management fee is generally a percentage of assets managed and is most often deducted directly from the accounts. The most common fee-related question asked of investment advisors is: "How much are my management fees?" It's a good question, but not the *right* question. If you have made this inquiry to your advisor, you can likely trust that the answer provided is the amount collected by your advisor's firm for his or her investment-related services (which might also include financial planning services). The problem with this question is that it doesn't tell you what you *really* want to know. What you need to—and should—know is how much you are paying *in total*.

To assess the total cost of your investments (or potential cost, if you are interviewing an investment advisor), we recommend asking these specific questions:

- What is my annual management fee and how is it assessed?

- Am I paying additional fees for any other services? If so, what services, how much, and how are the fees assessed?

- How much am I paying on the underlying investments (for example, *expense ratio*)?

- How much am I paying in transaction costs on each type of investment (for example, stocks, bonds, mutual funds), and who collects these commissions?

Total costs might range between 0.50% and 2.0%, varying based on a number of factors, some of which are specific to your situation and possibly out of your advisor's full control. So, be careful when comparing your costs to those paid by others and have a discussion with your advisor about how each fee component is set. Your advisor's value cannot be adequately assessed without a true understanding of cost.

Two $ense

Your advisor might quote fees in "basis points":
50 basis points = 0.50%; 100 basis points = 1.0%.

[35]
What's on the Menu?—Investing Styles

For some fortunate people, personal chefs are as customary as turkey on Thanksgiving. For most of us, however, a professionally commanded kitchen is out of our financial reach. While we can't make the case for fitting celebrity chef Bobby Flay into your budget, we can use a personal chef to help you understand two of the most common investment strategies: "passive" and "active." Your financial advisor might favor one approach over the other, or a combination of the two.

The terms passive and active refer to styles of investment management. As the name suggests, there is more activity in an active strategy, compared to a passive approach. But, what does that mean exactly?

Passive: Electing a passive investment strategy would be like hiring a personal chef who offered selections based on a preset list of ingredients, which rarely changes. Similarly, when choosing a passive *mutual fund* or *exchange traded fund (ETF)*, the manager of the fund will purchase investments of a preset menu or index. For example, the Vanguard 500 Index Fund (for illustrative purposes only) is invested in the 500 stocks that comprise the Standard & Poor's 500 Index (S&P 500), in equal weights (that is, if Apple represents 3% of the S&P 500, then the Vanguard fund will also hold 3% of Apple). The manager is not at liberty to look for other options and will only make changes to the underlying investments when an index changes (not often). Passive management is also referred to as "index investing" for its index-mimicking nature.

Active: Electing an active investment strategy, on the other hand, would be like hiring a personal chef who intends to make changes to the menu items based on price and seasonality of the ingredients, in addition to new ideas. Just as an active chef has the liberty to explore and make changes, so too does an active manager. He or she is not confined to a preset list or index and can make changes to the underlying investments when deemed appropriate.

So . . . which investing style is better? Both investment styles have their merits, and the debate continues about which approach is better. Just as there is no guarantee that you will actually like the active chef's new menu items, there is no guarantee an active manager will perform better than a passive one. In reality, some active strategies are better than passive strategies, and others are not. So, rather than make a definitive claim where we cannot, we will instead provide a couple of key considerations:

Cost: Due to the additional time and research it takes to seek out other ideas, the cost for active strategies is higher when compared to the passive counterparts. The average active mutual fund expense is between 0.65% and 1.30%, compared to 0.10% and 0.40% on passive funds and 0.50% on ETFs. The question of cost becomes one of expectation: Can you expect the autonomy of an active manager to be worth the additional expense?

Behavior: Index funds and ETFs are typically *market-cap* weighted and, as a result, the stocks and industries that perform well become an ever-larger portion of the index and the funds tracking it (think back to the "dotcom" bubble in the 1990s, at the end of which technology accounted for more than 55% of the Russell 1000 Growth Index). As a result, passive products tend to do best in momentum-driven markets. Alternatively, active managers maintain the flexibility to reduce the weight of a particular investment, if they have reason to believe momentum will not continue.

If you determine that you have a strong preference toward active or passive (or both) investing, find an advisor who aligns with this approach.

[36]
It's *Personal*—Asset Allocation

In the United States, one of the world's largest countries (pun intended), supplements have become quite popular. Admittedly, opinions about the effectiveness of supplements vary, but what we do know is that everyone is different and our body's needs are unique. The vitamin B your girlfriend takes might keep you up at night. The fish oil your Pilates instructor recommended might make you nauseated. Just as supplements should be tailored to your needs, so should your asset allocation. It's something personal that your advisor will create just for you.

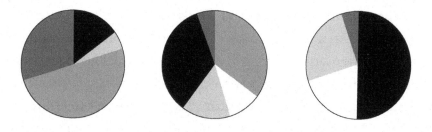

Asset allocation is the mix of investment types within a portfolio—most commonly, *stocks*, *bonds*, and cash. A primary goal for developing an asset allocation strategy is to manage risk through diversification. The proper asset allocation will depend on your financial situation, time horizon for using the funds, and your risk tolerance. Generally, when you are just starting out, your investment horizon is long, so your mix will include a greater percentage of riskier investments, like stocks. Eventually, it will slowly change to include a larger allocation to more conservative asset types, like bonds and/or cash. But, take caution when using general rules of thumb to determine how much you should have in various investment types (for example, "you should have 100 minus your age in stocks"), as these generalities ignore an above- or below-average appetite for risk, your unique needs from the investments, and they don't shed light on how to diversify among different types of stocks and bonds.

Throughout the past twenty years, the average individual investor has significantly underperformed both the stock and bond markets and has barely kept pace with inflation. Why? Because, like the wrong supplements, an inappropriate allocation could cause nausea and other financial side effects, leading to an emotional overreaction. Swings in your portfolio should solicit a manageable emotional response rather than cause you to sell an investment at a low point or buy at a high.

We're not saying that your mix won't change over time—it will and it should. What we are saying is that changes should be made when your *situation* changes and not because of an impulsive reaction to the market. Get your allocation right, ahead of time, so that you can stick with the right mix in any market environment.

[37]
It's Not a Tumor—Staying the Course

If you search online for "chronic headaches," you will be delivered words like *tumor*, *stroke*, and *infection*. Before accepting an untimely demise, you will likely make a call to your doctor for a second opinion. In a similar way, if you search online for "stock market," you might be met with headlines that include words like *plummets*, *sinks*, and *tumbles*. Turning to the Internet or various media outlets to draw conclusions about your financial well-being is a bit like diagnosing yourself with organ failure before seeing a doctor. The reality is, you won't really know until you seek the guidance of a professional. To avoid making what will likely be a poor investment decision during periods of heightened market volatility, seek a voice of reason, and meet with your financial advisor to discuss the following key points.

Portfolio Allocation: Major US stock market indices like the S&P 500 and Dow Jones Industrial Average (DJIA) dominate the headlines, but, unless your portfolio consists of *just* the 500 stocks in the S&P or *just* the 30 stocks in the Dow (and in exactly the same weightings as the respective index), the headlines will not reflect your reality. It is likely that your portfolio includes domestic and international stocks, bonds, an allocation to cash, and might also include other investment types, like private real estate or hedge funds. Review your portfolio with your advisor to understand the similarities and differences each investment type shares with major indices and corresponding variance in performance.

What It Means to You: Once you have brushed up on the makeup of your portfolio and have assessed your actual performance, evaluate what the performance means to you. Will a 5% decline in value today mean that you have to work longer or spend less, or is it immaterial? What about a 15% decline? If you are at or nearing retirement (or any other life event that requires distributions from your portfolio), consider using a bucket approach to determine how much you will spend in the short term, intermediate term, and long term. Work with your advisor to invest shorter-term funds more conservatively and longer-term funds more aggressively. This can help put investment returns into some context. Maybe the piece of your portfolio that is experiencing the most volatility represents funds that you aren't planning to touch for ten or more years. In this case, short-term fluctuations are most likely inconsequential over the long run.

Your Gut: Once you understand what it all means to you, take a step back to see if you are comfortable weathering the storm. Remember, the role of a professional is to help you make prudent and objective investment decisions. At the same time, your risk tolerance is subjectively personal. If your advisor believes that you can afford the level of volatility in your portfolio but you aren't sleeping at night, then consider a change. Sticking with an allocation with which you aren't comfortable will likely lead to reactive decisions at the wrong time. One way to ensure a disappointing investment experience is to start out too aggressive, sell when things get uncomfortable, and then reinvest more conservatively. It can be like digging a hole with a shovel and covering it back up with a spoon.

These conversations should help mute some of the market noise and make you feel more comfortable. It's quite possible you will learn from your advisor, and in the words of Arnold Schwarzenegger playing Detective John Kimble in *Kindergarten Cop:* "It's not a tumor!"

[38]
It's Contagious—The Economy in a Nutshell

At some point, while working with an advisor, you will have a conversation about the economy (whether you like it or not). Setting out to understand the world economy is a bit like organizing your closet. You know you should do it, but you just don't know where to start. Professional organizers recommend that you start small, doing a little bit each day. To help understand the economy in a nutshell, we recommend that you read on.

To begin, remember one simple thing: *income is contagious.* The more income you make, the more you spend, and the more you spend, the more income those on the receiving end of your spending make. In other words, income feeds off income. As we make more money, we buy more things, and this increase in demand increases prices. As certain asset prices rise, such as our houses and our investment accounts, we feel wealthier and have increased borrowing capacity, and so the spending cycle continues.

But, we don't just spend our income. No, no. We also *borrow* money to spend more. In fact, money spent using borrowed funds far exceeds that of traditional income, making credit one of the primary forces behind an economy's ebbs and flows. Cue the Federal Reserve System (the "Fed") and interest rates. The central bank of the United States—the Federal Reserve—controls the amount of credit available to consumers, and it has two tools with which to do so: interest rates and the money supply. Interest rates set the cost for borrowing, and the money supply affects the credit worthiness of potential borrowers.

Refer to the corresponding chart for how these tools work.

Goal	Tool	Direction	Influence
Increase Spending	Interest Rates	Low	Makes borrowing inexpensive and attractive.
	Money Supply	High	Increases income potential and creditworthiness, making borrowing easier.
Decrease Spending	Interest Rates	High	Makes borrowing expensive and unattractive.
	Money Supply	Low	Reduces income potential and creditworthiness, making borrowing more difficult.

While making more money and spending more money is good in theory, if there is too much money chasing too few goods and services, one dollar becomes less valuable (think: inflation).

Over long periods of time, debt payments can begin to exceed income and an economy might go through a period of reducing debt (deleverage). The most recent deleveraging in the United States occurred during the 2008 financial crisis. There are really four ways to reduce debt and increase income:

1. Spend less and apply more income to debt payments.

2. Default (do not pay) or restructure debts (pay less, reduce rate, or pay over a longer period of time).

3. Redistribute wealth by taking from those who still have it (in other words, increase taxes on the wealthy).

4. Print more money—by printing more money, the Fed can loan
    funds to the government, which, in turn, can funnel money
    into the hands of consumers through stimulus programs and
    unemployment benefits.

Each of these options has advantages and disadvantages, and there
is no single silver bullet. Ultimately, policymakers are tasked with
determining the best blend of these options to return an economy to
a healthy income-and-debt balance. Kind of makes cleaning out your
closet sound not so daunting, doesn't it?

End of Chapter Resources

Volatility Can Be Your Friend Video

Volatilty Can Be Your Friend Article

To access the end of chapter resources, go to
www.GetTheSense.com/Book-Resources.

Chapter 7

Insurance

As investment professionals, we are often tasked with reducing investment-related risk. But, there is risk of loss in all things of value—income, investments, and other personal property. In reality, underinsuring income or property can have a far greater financial impact on you and your loved ones than a temporary stock market decline. It would be a disservice to yourself to focus on creating a low-risk investment portfolio, while underinsuring your house or, worse, having no protection from a large liability claim. In this chapter, we will give you some food for thought to extend the risk conversation with your advisor beyond investments.

[39]
Buckle Up—Auto Insurance

So far, we have shared enlightening, relevant, knowledgeable, articulate, sound, beautiful, financial guidance . . . with zero bias, of course. While we strongly encourage you to heed each and every delicious morsel of our advice, the reality is . . . it's optional. That is, until now. When it comes to auto insurance, it is required by law that you purchase at least some coverage. So, we feel safe in making the assumption that you have auto insurance. We also feel safe in assuming that, unless you are an insurance agent, staring at your declarations page will not help you understand what it means or if you have the proper amount of protection. So, instead of recommending that you get coverage (we'll rest on the law for that), this entry will be dedicated to helping you decode your existing coverage and determine if you have enough.

When thinking about the risks of driving or owning a car, there are four main questions you likely want to know the answers to. Use our chart to determine which coverage provides the protection you are interested in, and review your insurance policy declarations page to check your coverage.

What You Want to Know . . .	Look at Your . . .	Make Note Of . . .	And, Ask . . .
What covers damage or theft of my car?	Collision Coverage and Comprehensive Coverage	Collision Coverage covers damage incurred in an accident. This will be required by a lender. Comprehensive Coverage covers damage or theft outside of an accident (think: tree falling on car).	Do I need **GAP insurance** to pay the difference between what my insurance company will pay and what I owe on a loan or lease?
What covers injury or damage I cause to others (people or cars)?	Bodily Injury Liability/ Property Damage/ Liability Coverage	Minimum coverage is required by state; amounts vary. Bodily Injury Liability Coverage covers injury-related expenses, such as medical, legal, loss of income, pain and suffering, and funeral incurred by an injured person (other than yourself; inside or outside of your car). Property Damage Liability Coverage covers damage to the other party's car or property. Coverage might be illustrated as: 100/300/50, which covers: per person injury/per accident total injury/property damage.	Is your coverage sufficient to cover injury-related expenses in your area? Consider potential loss of income and pain and suffering. Is your coverage high enough to cover the value of the types of cars you see on the road?

What You Want to Know . . .	Look at Your . . .	Make Note Of . . .	And, Ask . . .
What about my injuries and medical cost?	Medical Coverage	Available regardless of who is at fault and no deductible is required. Access to funds can come in handy to cover delays and restrictions by your health insurance company. If sufficient, it can cover health insurance deductibles and copays.	Is coverage sufficient to at least cover your health insurance deductible and copays?
What if the other driver does not have insurance?	Uninsured/ Underinsured Motorist	Might be required by state. Covers injury expenses incurred by you (and passengers) if you are hit by a driver with inadequate coverage, no coverage or a hit-and-run. Additional coverage might be added to cover property damage to your car (recommended).	Is your coverage at least as high as your other liability limits recommended?

Two $ense

Drivers who borrow your car might be covered automatically, or they might need to be listed as an insured driver on your policy, so know how your policy works before you lend.

[40]
There's No Place Like Home—Homeowners Insurance

After a long day at the office, chaotic carpool duties, a grueling workout, or maybe even an extended vacation, there is a place in your house that you crave. Whether it's that nook in your couch, your side of the bed, or the bathtub, it is your personal sanctuary, and it's worth protecting. Homeowners insurance protects your home—your refuge—and its contents from damage or theft. However, it is important to know that homeowners insurance options are not created equal, and there are key decisions that you must make to be sure that your coverage is adequate.

Primarily, you must choose the method by which your insurance company will pay you for a loss. Of course, the more they are expected to pay for a claim, the more you can expect to pay in premiums. Generally, your options will be as follows:

1. **Actual Cash Value** (not recommended): The insurer will pay you an amount equal to the value of damaged or stolen property, less depreciation (wear and tear). Since this method considers depreciation, the amount you are likely to receive is reduced. In other words, actual cash value (ACV) is the amount you would receive if you tried to sell the property or item to someone

else. If you are insured for ACV, we recommend shopping for more comprehensive coverage, such as Replacement Cost or Extended Replacement Cost, described below.

2. **Replacement Cost:** Preferred over ACV, this method does not take depreciation into account. With it, you will be reimbursed for the amount it will cost to rebuild your house or replace an item of similar quality, up to the limit of coverage in your policy.

3. **Extended Replacement Cost:** As the name suggests, this form of coverage works in a manner similar to Replacement Cost, with a little extra. With Extended Replacement Cost, the insurance company might provide for an additional 25–50% of your coverage limit to rebuild your house or replace an item of similar quality. It's important to note that this additional protection requires you to keep the insurance company informed of any property improvements to ensure that your stated policy limit is adequate.

Be careful in comparing the coverage on your house to its current market value. In certain areas, land is a large part of a property's market value and, if your home were to burn down, you wouldn't need to replace the land. Considering improvements, changes in building codes, increases in construction costs, and other factors in rebuilding, there really is no correlation between current market value and costs to rebuild. So, work with your insurance agent every few years to make sure your coverage is adequate.

Take a Ride-r! Standard coverage limits available for certain high-value items, like jewelry, furs, collectibles, and fine art might not be sufficient to cover their actual value. Scheduling these items on a personal property *rider* will allow you to secure additional coverage, at an additional cost. It is a great idea to take photos or a video of these special items to document proof of ownership. A picture is worth 1,000 words . . . or potentially $1,000.

[41]
Million-Dollar Baby—Personal Liability (Umbrella) Insurance

Parents of teenage drivers; landlords; pool, boat, or trampoline owners; pet owners; and, well, everyone else, listen up! It's possible that you are just a party foul or driveway fall away from losing everything. You might think that having auto  and homeowners insurance is all you need to protect yourself from money-grubbing plaintiffs, but you'd be wrong, which is the reason you need a personal liability (umbrella) policy. An umbrella policy is designed to offer an extension of coverage above and beyond where your homeowners or auto policies fall short. Think you don't need an umbrella because you have nothing to keep dry? Think again. What you are worth today isn't all that you have to protect. A claim greater than your existing auto or homeowners coverage can allow a claimant to garnish your future income. *Ouch.*

Let's say you run a red light and hit a surgeon crossing the street. The cost to cover injuries and loss of wages amounts to $750,000 but you only have $100,000 in auto liability coverage. An umbrella policy would step up to cover the extra $650,000 claim against you, including legal fees.

Your current net worth and future financial security are well worth the cost of this relatively cheap coverage. A $1 million policy might be about $200 a year. Over time, it's important to make sure that your coverage keeps up with your net worth and income. If you don't have an umbrella policy, make the call to your property and casualty insurance agent. It could be the most valuable call you ever make.

Two $ense

Coordination of liability coverage is key. Review your policies
to ensure that your underlying auto and home liability limits
are not above the minimum required by your liability policy.
Don't pay for more than what you need!

[42]
The Goose or the Golden Egg?—Disability Insurance

What is more valuable . . . a goose or its golden eggs? The obvious answer is the goose, for, without it, there would be no eggs. Now, unless you are Willy Wonka, it's unlikely that you'll be faced with this decision in real life, but, there is a similar decision that most employed individuals should make. Think of your ability to earn income as your "goose," and think of your house, cars, jewelry, art collection, or any other valuables as your golden "eggs." While most of us will work with a licensed property and casualty agent to ensure that our valuables are adequately insured, less often we work with a professional to ensure that our income is protected.

The best way to protect your income is with disability insurance. If you become disabled and are no longer able to work, an insurance company will provide income for a period of time. Disability policies will generally replace 50–70% of your income. Here is what you need to know about disability insurance:

Do I need to get coverage? It depends. If you or your loved ones are relying on your earned income to cover your lifestyle, then the answer is yes, you need disability coverage.

How do I get it? First, look to your employer. Many employers provide group disability insurance to employees. A typical group arrangement will provide three to six months of short-term disability coverage (generally after sick pay has been exhausted), followed by long-term benefits up to age 65 or recovery, if earlier. Group coverage is generally less expensive than getting an individual policy and can be easier to obtain without requiring medical underwriting. On the other hand, the benefit might only insure a portion of your salary (perhaps not your bonus), and you might not be able to take the coverage with you if you leave your employer.

Be aware that disability policies have a monthly benefit cap. Your group policy might replace up to 60% of income, but be subject to a $5,000 per month cap. The cap amount might be far less than 60% of actual income. So, if your employer has a group plan, you might need an individual policy to get the maximum amount of coverage. Although an individual policy is more expensive than group coverage and will typically require medical underwriting, it will go wherever you go and coverage can be customized to insure various sources of income like self-employment, salary, and bonus.

What else? Know if your policies have an "own occupation" rider. This rider will provide coverage if you can no longer work in your existing occupation, even if you are able to secure employment in a different field. Last, when determining the amount of coverage you need, keep in mind that benefits received from an individual policy or a group policy paid for by you are generally not taxable, whereas group coverage paid for by an employer will be subject to income tax.

Two $ense

Short-term disability insurance might also provide coverage for work leave needed due to pregnancy.

"So much time and so little to do. Wait a minute. Strike that. Reverse it. Thank you."

—Willy Wonka

[43]
More Mortals—Life Insurance

There is a special place in our brains where we file certain thoughts or feelings that we don't want to deal with. You might be storing your most embarrassing moment, last heart break, worst mistake, or, maybe, that corner of your garage that desperately needs organizing. If you are like most people, the thought of your own mortality is likely also tucked away somewhere in there. Death is just something that we mortals don't like to think about, nevermind plan for. While pondering your own mortality is uncomfortable, the thought of loved ones struggling financially due to lack of planning, should be more unsettling. So, we are asking you to tap into that part of your brain and think about it. Ultimately, to determine your unique insurance needs, we recommend working with your financial advisor.

Life insurance pays a tax-free death benefit to a named beneficiary following the death of the insured. If there is anyone in your life who depends on you financially, then you should have life insurance for as long as you will be depended on. In addition to replacing lost income, insurance can be used to pay off existing debts, or provide for other financial goals and priorities, such as college.

For young families, we recommend having enough life insurance that the investment growth alone could replace your after-tax income. For example, if your after-tax income is $75,000, assuming a 5% investment return, $1.5 million of insurance will be sufficient ($1.5 million x 5% = $75,000). While the result might seem to overestimate the need, the coverage should yield an amount that will maintain your family's lifestyle and provide a cushion for unexpected expenses or lower-than-expected investment performance. Given its low cost, this coverage is likely to be term insurance for the number of years until retirement.

Capital Preservation Method After-Tax Income Need / 5%

Income Replacement Calculation Insurance Need

$50,000 / 5% = $1 million

$100,000 / 5% = $2 million

$200,000 / 5% = $4 million

$300,000 / 5% = $6 million

For families nearing retirement, the need for life insurance might decrease, as the number of income-producing years becomes fewer. Multiplying the number of years you expect to work, by your annual after-tax income, should provide enough coverage to allow your survivors to cover both expenses and savings until retirement. Keep in mind that this might fall short if your death would cause a loss in one or more retirement income sources (think: pension).

Two $ense

It's not only necessary to consider insurance for the household breadwinner. If you are a stay-at-home parent, making it possible for your spouse to work, there is definitely financial dependence on you also!

[44]
If I Knew Then—Long-Term Care Insurance

Wisdom is defined in part as the quality of having experience. By definition, only after an experience will we become wise. This is why only our older, ahem, wiser selves can look back to our youth and say, "Wear sunscreen," "Take care of your body," "Don't go out with Chad," or "Prioritize date night." When it comes to planning for your future, rather than relying on your own wisdom—which comes after-the-fact—why not piggyback on the experiences of others instead? Although your twenty-year-old self couldn't see the inevitable damage of no sunscreen, your current self can wise up to an issue your future self is highly likely to experience: the need for long-term care insurance.

Long-term care insurance provides benefits for nursing-home care, home-health care, personal or adult day care for individuals with a chronic or disabling condition that need assistance with two or more *activities of daily living (ADLs)*, think bathing, dressing, and eating. Of people turning age 65, 70% will expect to use some form of long-term care during their lives. The healthier you are, the greater the chance that you will need help over your (expected) longer lifetime. Yet, creating a game plan for long-term care is something that many of us don't want to face.

We get it. It's hard to imagine being dependent on others for our own care. Instead, we plan for other, more palatable expenses, like college funding. Although long-term care costs vary by state, in certain states, like California, the cost of full-time assistance could be more than a four-year education. Absent proper planning, the burden of care will fall on children and loved ones—both emotionally and financially. A plan to help cover the financial costs should be just as important as college funding.

A long-term care plan might include self-insuring, if you have enough income or assets to cover the expense, transferring the risk to an insurance company by purchasing a long-term care policy, or a combination of both. To allow time to accumulate assets dedicated to this need and to help keep insurance costs down, we recommend that you begin planning for long-term care needs in your early fifties. Don't let your seventy-year-old self say, "If I knew then, what I know now" about long-term care.

[45]
The Art of Science—Health Insurance Basics

Almost all financial decisions come with trade-offs, making decisions more art than science. This could not be truer than when it comes

to selecting a health insurance plan. Choosing a health insurance plan is a decision that most of us revisit every year—and the struggle is real . . . every year. The health insurance trade-off is one between premiums and out-of-pocket expenses; in exchange for lower premiums comes higher deductibles and a larger share of costs for care. The ideal plan really depends on how much care you are going to need, making it challenging for anyone who doesn't have a crystal ball. Although we are unable to create certainty where there isn't any, we can help you think through the process and help you understand some key concepts when selecting your plan.

What Should I Know before Selecting a Plan? To start, it is helpful to understand the type of experience you might expect with a given plan type. The two most common plan types are HMOs and PPOs (other, less common plan types include *POSs* and *EPOs*).

HMOs: Health maintenance organizations provide coverage only when care is received within their network (think Kaiser Permanente). Some plans require insureds to be seen by a primary care physician for treatment, before being seen by a specialist. Because HMO coverage is limited to a known network of providers who have accepted the insurance company's negotiated rates, premiums tend to be lower than other plan types.

PPOs: Preferred provider organizations do not require members to seek care from in-network providers, but there is a financial incentive to do so, because benefits are greater in-network. Unlike HMOs, PPOs do not require a primary care physician referral before members are seen by a specialist. Because PPOs provide greater flexibility and provider access, premiums tend to be higher than their HMO counterparts.

Next, since selecting a plan is all about keeping expenses down, it's important to understand the costs that you might incur and how they work. Here are the different ways you can expect to share in healthcare related costs:

Deductible: This is the amount you must pay (in addition to premiums) before insurance will kick in. It usually ranges between $500 and $5,000. Still, certain services might be fully or partially covered by your insurance company, even before your full deductible is met. It is important to know that copayments (see below) are generally not applied toward deductibles, and only amounts paid for *eligible* medical services and prescriptions count. If your insurance company doesn't cover a particular treatment or drug, the amount you pay will not be applied toward your deductible. Also, understand that once your deductible is met, you will still be responsible for a portion of costs incurred by way of copayments and coinsurance, described here.

Copayment: This is a flat fee that you pay for doctor visits and prescriptions. Copayment amounts might vary based on the nature of your visit (for example, primary care or specialist) and drug (for example, generic or brand name, pick-up or mail order). In most cases, copayments are not required for preventative care visits that are in-network.

Coinsurance: This is your share of the *allowed* costs of a covered service and typically ranges between 10%-30%. Allowed amount is an important concept to remember so that you aren't surprised by out-of-pocket costs. For example, if your plan allows for $500 per day for hospital visits, and your total cost after a four-day stay is $2,600, the allowed amount is only $2,000 ($500 x four days). If your coinsurance is 20%, you will be responsible for 20% of $2,000, or $400, plus the full $600 of disallowed charges.

Out-of-pocket maximum: This is the maximum amount you could pay in a year and includes deductibles, coinsurance, and copays. Once your out-of-pocket maximum is met, your insurance company will cover 100% of all healthcare-related costs.

Ultimately, you will pay a premium to have insurance. When you need care, you will pay more of the cost of care until your deductible is met. Once your total costs (excluding copays) reaches your deductible amount, your insurance company will pay for a larger chunk. Once your copays, deductibles, and/or coinsurance payments reach the annual out-of-pocket maximum, your insurance company will pay 100% of any additional costs incurred.

How Do I Choose? Now, for the hard part. Follow the below steps to help you think through the process.

1. **Make sure your doctor accepts the plan.** Call the doctors you would like to continue working with and make sure they accept the plan you are considering.

2. **Make sure frequently used prescriptions are covered.** Call the insurance providers to make sure that at least your most frequently used prescriptions are covered.

3. **Think through your healthcare needs.** Review the care you incurred during the past year and consider any changes that you expect in the coming year. If you believe that your needs will stay the same and you didn't meet your full deductible, perhaps you can consider a higher deductible plan in exchange for lower premiums. If you were close to or exceeded your deductible, you might consider a higher premium plan in exchange for a lower deductible. Remember that once you meet your deductible and the insurance company steps in, cost sharing comes into play. So, for lower deductible plans, it makes sense to seek a plan with lower coinsurance amounts (your share).

4. **Determine total cost and risk appetite.** To determine how much of your dollars could be on the line, multiply your

monthly premium amount by twelve and add it to your out-of-pocket maximum. This is how much you could pay, in total, in a given year. Depending on your appetite for risk, you might opt for a lower premium policy with a higher risk of coming out of pocket for extensive care or, you might take the more conservative approach, paying higher premiums, and transferring more of the risk to your insurer. If you are comfortable rolling the dice with a high-deductible plan, work with your benefits department on incorporating a **health savings account (HSA)** with your plan. In 2017, an HSA allows you to set aside $3,400 for an individual and $6,750 for a family plan on a pretax basis to cover out-of-pocket medical expenses.

Only in hindsight will you know if you chose the *best* plan. Still, regardless of the plan you choose, it will provide coverage to protect against catastrophic health insurance costs, which is really why you are insuring in the first place.

Two $ense

If your employer offers a healthcare *flexible spending account (FSA)*, you might save money on copayments, contact lens solution, flu shots, and many more healthcare-related expenses. In 2017, up to $2,600 can be set aside to a FSA on a pretax basis. The list of covered costs is extensive, making it more likely to cover expenses you will incur. If you're going to pay for them anyway, why not get a tax benefit for doing so?

Chapter 8

Estate Planning

In the words of author Susan Covel Alpert, "The only thing worse than talking about death is NOT talking about it." In this chapter, we will be taking you on a journey to prepare for the financial component that most closely relates to the heart: an estate plan. Think of an estate plan as your blueprint for what happens after your incapacitation or passing. Imagine your family making difficult medical decisions on your behalf, handling important financial transactions, caring for your children, or spending time and money for the court to make decisions for you. Although a will is important, it is just one of the five important pieces of a bigger plan that makes a difficult time a bit easier for loved ones. Because home is where the heart is, what better analogy to use than building a home?

[46]
Lay the Foundation—Living Trust

Every dream home starts with a host of ideas that culminate in a vision that leads to the pouring of the foundation. Similarly, every estate plan starts with a lot of thought that ultimately shapes your *living trust.* Think of your living trust as laying the foundation for your family. It is the source through which you will communicate with loved ones your wishes related to managing and transferring property after your death or incapacity. A living trust will be revocable (amendable), as long as you have capacity to make changes, but becomes irrevocable (set in stone) after your death.

While a will might also be used to communicate these wishes, a trust is preferred in many states, because property directed by the trust passes outside the often expensive and time-consuming process of *probate.* If you don't have a will or living trust, your state's default rules determine who receives your assets that do not have beneficiary designations or are not jointly owned. It is less likely that the default rules will pass properly according to your wishes if you are unmarried or have a blended family.

Just like when laying the foundation of a new home, there are additional steps that must be taken after drafting a trust to complete the job. For your trust to direct assets, you must fund the trust by transferring title of such assets to it. Titling assets accordingly lets financial institutions and your loved ones know that there is a thoughtfully constructed rule book that needs to be followed.

Two $ense

Keep in mind that while certain assets, such as retirement plans and life insurance, have beneficiary designations, others do not. Before getting your will or trust in place, you might be able to protect your wishes with regard to these other assets by establishing transfer on death (TOD) instructions on the accounts. TOD rules vary by state, so work with your financial advisor to make sure all of your accounts have allowable designations.

[47]
Whom Will You Choose?—Will

Once you have officially "broken ground" with a trust, there are still some pieces that need to be put into place to complete your estate plan. Continuing with our home-building analogy, think of drafting a will as similar to choosing a general contractor; you will choose a key person to carry out some important tasks to ensure that nothing falls through the cracks.

A will is a legally enforceable document that might be used to communicate your wishes related to managing and transferring property after your death or incapacity. But, in states like California, Arizona, and Nevada where probate is difficult and assets are primarily distributed through a trust, you still need a will for other important reasons. Your will nominates guardians for your children, an executor to funnel assets left out of the trust into the trust, and a conservator to act on your incapacity. Without a will, the court—a stranger—will decide who is best fit to act as guardian for your children, how assets not directed by beneficiary designation or trust will pass to survivors, and who will act as your conservator.

In an effort to avoid an awkward scene similar to the one in the 2010 movie Life as We Know It, be sure to ask those you want to serve as key players if they are willing to take on the responsibility and provide them with copies of key documents appointing them to act. Just as clearly as your contractor knows what is expected of him, your loved ones should know what is expected of them.

[48]
Your Contractors—Power of Attorney

By creating a trust and a will, you have planned well in the event of your death. However, a complete estate plan also includes arrangements in the event of your incapacitation.

Your healthcare power of attorney (also known as an advanced healthcare directive) names the person(s) you have chosen to make healthcare-related decisions on your behalf and who is responsible for ensuring that all care meets your wishes. This document also allows you to let others know what medical treatment you want, to specify your preferences about pain relief if you are terminally ill or permanently unconscious, to express your wishes about prolonging life under certain circumstances, and to outline your wishes about organ donation and other final arrangements.

Your power of attorney for financial matters allows you to authorize someone else to make financial decisions if you are unable to do so.

While the successor trustee of your trust will be able to handle a good portion of financial matters, some actions, such as signing tax returns or transacting on retirement accounts, require specific appointment. Among other things, your appointed "agent" might be delegated to pay your everyday expenses, watch over your investments, file your taxes, and/or collect retirement plan or insurance benefits.

It is important to update your power of attorney document periodically to ensure that no one is left doubting that it is the most current version. Some financial institutions will not honor documents that are older than ten years. Also, just like other key players in your estate plan, it's important to ask those who you would like to serve if they are willing to take on the responsibility and, if so, provide them with copies of your most recent documents.

Two $ense

So that your appointed agent(s) can make informed decisions about your healthcare, it is important to release your medical information using a Health Insurance Portability and Accountability Act of 1996 (HIPAA) release form, which should be incorporated by your attorney. Review your plan to make sure this important document is in place.

[49]
What Not to Nuke—Funding Your Trust

If you've ever left a piece of foil on a dish, set chocolate chips on fire, or exploded eggs in the microwave, then you know that some things just shouldn't go in there. In this way, your living trust is a lot like a microwave; directing certain assets to it could have unintended consequences.

Review the considerations here before putting all of your assets in the name of your trust or naming it as a beneficiary.

IRAs/Retirement Plans: IRAs and retirement plan accounts cannot be titled to the name of your trust. Naming the trust as the beneficiary is the alternate way for the trust to direct the disposition of these assets but, be careful! Naming your trust as the beneficiary of your 401(k), IRA, or other retirement plan might be a big mistake (big, huge)! The trust might require beneficiaries to take everything out of the plan as taxable income within five years of your death, rather than allowing them to stretch distributions—and ordinary income tax— throughout their lifetimes.

Does this mean that I should never name my trust as the beneficiary of a retirement plan? No. You might need the trust to control how your retirement assets are received by minor beneficiaries or beneficiaries with creditor, spending, or substance-abuse problems. It is possible to name the trust as a beneficiary without the negative consequences previously mentioned, if you are using a trust specifically created for that purpose. Not sure? Ask your attorney for specific beneficiary directions and check whether who you have named as beneficiary of your retirement plans matches the instructions provided.

Nothing: Putting the wrong things in your microwave can create a mess, but putting nothing in it can also end in a blow-up (it's true, don't try it). In the same way, failing to fund your trust is a great way to ensure that it doesn't function properly. Funding a trust is the process of retitling assets and property into the name of the trust. It's your way of telling the world: "If something happens to me, look to this trust for my instructions on what to do with this piece of property." Although it is rare that we would forget to put our meal into the microwave before starting it, failing to fund a living trust is one of the most common estate-planning mistakes. Again, work with your attorney to retitle property, as instructed.

Two $ense

Common assets titled in trust include real estate, business interests, and some cash and investment accounts, but it's not for everything.

Extra $ense

The title to your house might revert to joint or individual title following a refinance, so be sure to retitle it to your trust. Also, make sure your trust is named as an additional insured on your homeowners policy.

[50]
Adulting—Trustee Designations

Something has happened. Your dinnerware set finally matches, you've graduated from box wine to bottles, you're making your own dentist appointments and, despite your best efforts, you have started to channel your mother. You have become an adult. Just when you think you've got adulting down, you learn that someone has named you as *trustee* of their trust. *Gulp.* Among everyone they know, they think YOU are responsible enough to make sure their money or property does what it's supposed to do if they can't be in control. Before regretting every responsible decision you've never made, remember that it is an honor to be chosen as trustee. It's also a moral and legal responsibility, so, here are some tips to make sure you are up for the task.

Ask When. In most cases, your responsibility as trustee won't start today, but rather at some future time as a backup. The most common type of trust is a revocable living trust, which controls how an individual or couple's property is used for their lifetimes and how it is passed to loved ones after they die—cue you as the *successor trustee.* Your role is to take over the control and disposition of property, if the trust creators die or become incapacitated. If the trust is an *irrevocable trust* instead, your responsibilities as trustee might start immediately or again at a later time as a successor (future) trustee.

Ask Why. You are likely being asked to manage and distribute assets for your friend or family member if something happens to them and to distribute property to care for their children or other loved ones. If the trust is irrevocable, it more likely has a specific purpose for its creation, such as providing for education or benefits to someone with special needs. It's not asking too much to want to know generally who the trust benefits and the primary purpose of the trust. If you are being asked to serve immediately, this is clearly an area where you should feel free to ask any questions.

Ask What. As trustee, it is important to know what assets the trust controls. Odds are, if the trust is a living trust, it controls your friend/family member's house, investments, and life insurance, but it could also own an interest in a business or rental real estate. Trust assets change over time, so if you are a successor trustee, you might just ask if there is anything you should know about what property the trust holds now. If you are being asked to serve as trustee immediately, you'll definitely need to know exactly what the trust will own, because you will be legally responsible to manage those assets.

Ask Where. If you are a successor trustee, you should minimally know where to get a copy of the trust, should something happen to the current acting trustee. If you are being asked to serve immediately, you'll need a copy of the trust now, as the trust document is your written instruction on how to manage and distribute assets to beneficiaries.

Grab Your Sticky Notes. There will be a lot of legalese in the trust, but there is also clear language, so get out your sticky notes and dig in. You can and should ask the estate attorney to explain anything you do not understand.

Get Serious and Seek Help. As a trustee, you are held to a fiduciary standard of care. That means you'll need to put the beneficiaries' needs above your own, treat beneficiaries fairly, protect and invest the trust assets prudently, keep records, and file tax returns. The trust will likely allow you to use assets to pay for professional help. Most trustees work with an accountant, an estate attorney, and a financial advisor.

Know Your Options. You don't have to be an attorney, CPA, or a financial wizard to be a trustee, and your friend or family wouldn't have named you as trustee if they didn't think you were up to the task. It is a big responsibility, though, so if you aren't comfortable, you can decline the position. If you are comfortable but worry that your sentiment might change as life changes, know that you can later decline to serve or resign in the future.

End of Chapter Resources

Vital Family Information Packet
When a Loved One Passes Checklist

To access the end of chapter resources, go to
www.GetTheSense.com/Book-Resources.

Chapter 9

Taxes

Making sense of the tax code is a bit like trying to understand Madonna's wardrobe selections. It's no wonder that perhaps more than any other personal finance concept, there are misconceptions about how taxes actually work. We could easily get carried away with boring facts about tax. Instead, we hope to have some fun with the most important and relevant information relating to taxes. Yes, we really did just use the words "fun" and "taxes" in the same sentence.

Before you read on, we have just one minor request . . . don't shoot the messenger!

[51]
Patience Is Not an IRS Virtue—Tax Refunds and Penalties

"The best way to teach your kids about taxes is by eating 30 percent of their ice cream."

—Bill Murray

Income tax is—perhaps more than any other financial aspect of our lives—emotional. When your CPA tells you that you are getting a refund, you likely feel joyful and victorious. When you are told that you owe more tax, on the other hand, you probably feel angry and defeated. When preparing for tax season, try to avoid the emotional roller coaster by coming to terms with a couple of misperceptions about tax.

For starters, know that patience is a virtue that the IRS does not have. Rather than paying all taxes due at once, taxpayers must abide by a pay-as-you-go system via paycheck withholdings and/or estimated payments. So, April 15 isn't really the due date for taxes; it's more of a "settle up" date. If your withholdings or estimated payments throughout the year are not sufficient to cover the taxes you owe, you will pay more. If paid in excess, you will get a refund.

Ultimately, receiving a tax refund is no more a gift than owing more tax is a penalty. Getting excited about a tax refund is a bit like asking someone to hold your wallet and then being ecstatic when they give it back to you. The money was always yours to begin with. A tax refund is just that—a return of your money. Getting down about owing more tax is like being upset that you had to give someone else their wallet back. It was never really yours to spend.

Rather than loaning the government extra money throughout the year, decrease your withholdings to keep control of your funds. Instead of spending the extra cash, set up an automatic savings or investment plan. On the flip side, the IRS is impatient and gets angry when it doesn't get what it wants. Underpaying by a large enough amount can result in an underpayment penalty. So, increase your withholdings to avoid this penalty. Ideally, try to avoid large refunds or underpayments and stay off of the emotional tax ride.

[52]
The Bracket Ride—Income Tax Brackets

One of the simpler tax facts to figure out is your federal income tax bracket. Take a quick look at line 43 of Form 1040 and refer to the brackets provided by the IRS. We'll wait . . .

In 2017, if you were married, filed a joint tax return, and had *taxable income* of $100,000 (line 43), you fall into the 25% marginal income tax bracket. Despite a popular belief, this does not mean that every dollar of income is taxed at 25%. No, no. This would be entirely too simple for the Internal Revenue Code. Fortunately, this tax twist works to our advantage. Instead of being fully taxed at the highest marginal rate, income gets to ride through each bracket. Think of tax brackets like steps on a ladder. To get to the top, your income passes through each rung and is taxed along the way. The amount of income each step will carry before moving up to the next bracket depends on your filing status (think Facebook relationship status: single, married, or, it really does get complicated).

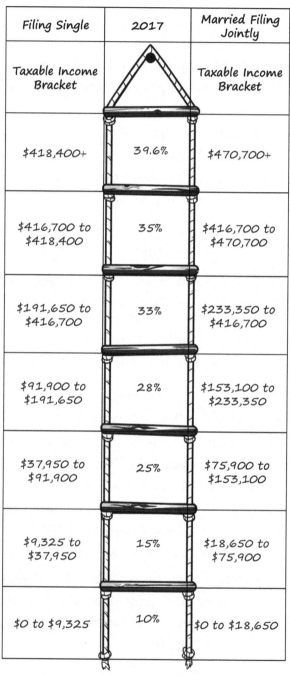

Filing Single	2017	Married Filing Jointly
Taxable Income Bracket		Taxable Income Bracket
$418,400+	39.6%	$470,700+
$416,700 to $418,400	35%	$416,700 to $470,700
$191,650 to $416,700	33%	$233,350 to $416,700
$91,900 to $191,650	28%	$153,100 to $233,350
$37,950 to $91,900	25%	$75,900 to $153,100
$9,325 to $37,950	15%	$18,650 to $75,900
$0 to $9,325	10%	$0 to $18,650

Annual tax brackets
subject to change

In the 2017 married filing joint example above, the first $18,650 of income is taxed at 10%, then income up to $75,900 is taxed at 15%, and so on. So, your ***marginal income tax rate*** doesn't tell you how every dollar is taxed, but it does tell you the rate at which your next dollar of income will be taxed, which makes it important to know. Do yourself a favor and don't focus on your marginal rate, because it doesn't represent your true tax rate. Instead, divide your total tax (line 63) by your taxable income (yep, still line 43) to determine your ***effective tax rate*** (or average rate).

[53]
Why's He Getting All My Money?!—FICA Tax

F•R•I•E•N•D•S fans will recall when Rachel received her first hard-earned paycheck from Central Perk only to find that some guy named "FICA" had taken a decent chunk (in addition to federal and state taxes). Well, FICA is also getting a cut of your pay, likely near 8%, so we want you to know where your money is going . . .

First, FICA stands for the Federal Insurance Contributions Act, which established the tax that you and your employer pay to fund the Social Security and Medicare programs that support us in old age. Your employer withholds 1.45% of all your wages for Medicare, 6.2% on your first $127,200 (in 2017) of wages for Social Security, and your employer contributes the same amounts on your behalf.

Knowing that you shouldn't have the 6.2% withheld for Social Security on more than your first $127,200 of wages is important for those of you who have side gigs or switch jobs mid-year. If you withhold from both jobs, you could end up overpaying. While you can request a refund if you overpay, you can avoid this interest-free loan to the government just by making sure you let your multiple employers know what's already been withheld.

[54]
Some Relief—Reducing Taxable Income

Yes, it is possible to save on taxes if you get married, have a child, or buy a house. Commitment-phobes or not, we would argue that none of these are worth exploring for the sake of tax savings alone. There are other, much easier, ways of reducing your tax bill that don't require a walk down the aisle or a waddle to the hospital.

Tax "Discounts"

Exemptions: Exemptions are like little gifts from the IRS, allowing most taxpayers to avoid tax on a small amount of income each year. In 2017, as long as you file a return, you will get an exemption for you and your *dependents* of up to $4,050 per person. For example, if you are married with two children, your exemption amount would be $16,200 ($4,050 x four). Note that if your *adjusted gross income (AGI)* exceeds a certain dollar amount, your exemption amount might be reduced or eliminated.

Deductions: Deductions are essentially costs that you incur in life that the IRS allows you to subtract from income. There are two groups of deductions: those taken to arrive at adjusted gross income (AGI) (line 37 of Form 1040) and those taken to further reduce AGI to arrive at taxable income (line 43 of Form 1040). Deductions taken to arrive at AGI are referred to as "above-the-line" deductions. Those taken to further reduce income are referred to as "below-the-line" (AGI, line 37, being the proverbial line, of course). The good news is, you get to take both . . . maybe.

Above-the-line deductions include student loan interest, IRA or self-employed retirement plan contributions, self-employed health insurance premiums, and paying alimony. If incurred, these expenses can be deducted from income by most anyone (some exceptions apply for high-income earners). The rule for these deductions is, *take 'em*. Take 'em if you can, because reducing AGI can have a positive impact on many things, including retirement account contributions and eligibility, and health-insurance premiums.

Below-the-line deductions might be a standard amount or an itemized amount, if higher. Taxpayers must tally up certain deductions and compare them to the standard deduction, which is the minimum amount allowed by the IRS. Itemized deductions include mortgage interest, state and local income taxes, charitable donations, car registration, property taxes, certain out-of-pocket medical expenses, and a few others. In 2017, the standard deduction is $6,350 per person ($12,700 for joint filers). If your itemized deductions are greater than the standard, take 'em! If not, use the standard deduction instead. Note that your deductions might also be reduced or eliminated if your AGI exceeds a certain threshold.

Tax Credits

Credits: Credits are the best way to reduce tax, because they are a dollar-for-dollar offset against your tax liability. Credits include the Child and Dependent Care Credit, Adoption Credit, Child Tax

Credit, American Opportunity Tax Credit, Lifetime Learning Tax Credit, Plug-in Electric Drive Motor Vehicle Credit, Residential Energy Efficient Property Credit, and Low-Income Housing Credit. Because they are so beneficial, credits are much harder to qualify for, and income usually needs to be fairly low to take advantage of most credits.

Two $ense

Good news! Contributions made on a pretax basis to 401(k)s or other company retirement plans also reduce taxable income. This is because wages reported by your employer on Form W-2 are already reduced by the amount of these contributions.

[55]
The Long and the Short of It—Capital Gains

Certain things happen with age that we don't even realize. Our hormones change, our brains get smaller, and fat literally vanishes from the bottom of our feet (yes, it's true). We also begin to accumulate capital assets, as we become more financially "mature." Capital assets include items such as real estate, cars, stocks, bonds, and other investment types, such as mutual funds and ETFs. Apart from certain personal use items, like cars or boats, the goal for most capital assets is that their value will increase over time. Remember, this is the tax chapter so you might get where we're going here. Just like with income, when you make money on a capital asset, the IRS wants its cut.

Note: Tax on capital gains does not apply to capital assets held inside IRAs or other retirement plans, which are sheltered from the taxation described below.

If you sell an asset for more than you paid for it, you will realize a capital gain. If you sell it for less than what you paid, you will realize a capital loss. The operative word here is sell. There will be no tax on your assets appreciating in value, until you *sell* them.

Capital gains and losses are classified as long term or short term. If you hold an asset for more than one year before selling it, the capital gain or loss is long term. If your holding period is one year or less, the gain or loss will be considered short term. This categorization matters for tax purposes. Gains realized on assets held for more than a year are taxed at lower rates than short-term assets (more on this below).

To determine your gain or loss in a given year, know that gains and losses in the same year are netted against each other. For example, assume that you make the following transactions in a year: Sold stock A for a long-term gain of $100; sold bond B for a short-term gain of $25; sold mutual fund C for a short-term loss of -$100; sold ETF D for a long-term gain of $500. To determine your net capital gain or loss for the year, start by grouping the types together, as shown.

Sold stock A for a **long-term** gain of $100

Sold bond B for a **short-term** gain of $25

Sold ETF D for a **long-term** gain of $500

Sold mutual fund C for a **short-term** loss of -$100

The initial result is a long-term capital gain of $600 and a short-term capital loss of -$75. Subtract the loss from the gain and your end result is a net, long-term, capital gain of $525. The tax rate schedule for long-term capital gains is different from that of ordinary income, but the amount of taxable income you have does affect your capital gain tax rate. For most taxpayers, the tax rate applied to long-term gains will be between 0% and 15%. In 2017, the maximum, long-term, capital gain, tax rate is 23.8%. Compared to the maximum *income* tax rate of 39.6%, you can see the preferential tax treatment given to long-term investments. Short-term capital gains, on the other hand, are considered ordinary income for tax purposes and are taxed as such.

Once again is realized and the appropriate amount of tax is paid, you can mostly consider it a wrap. Losses, however, linger for tax purposes, which is a good thing. Capital losses that exceed gains in a given year can be used to offset income and future gains. Let's say, for example, that, in year one, you sell a bad real estate investment for a $75,000 loss, while gains on other assets for the year total $10,000. Your net position is a $65,000 loss. The IRS allows you to use $3,000 of this loss to reduce ordinary income for the year and any remaining losses can be used to offset future gains. Let's assume that in year two, you have net gains of $25,000. You might use your remaining loss carry forward of $62,000 ($65,000 - $3,000) to fully offset this gain, plus another $3,000 to offset ordinary income. Headed into year three, you still have $34,000 in losses to be applied toward future years ($62,000 - $25,000 - $3,000).

Two $ense

If you realize a gain on the sale of your primary residence, you can exclude from taxation $250,000 if filing single, or $500,000 for joint filers. Losses from the sale of certain personal-use property, such as your houses or car, cannot be used to offset gains or reduce income.

[56]
Final Tidbits—Tax Facts

We know what you're thinking . . . *more on taxes?* Yes, but these final tax tidbits are common enough that a chapter on tax would just not be complete without them. We're willing to bet that at least one of these tax situations will be relevant to you at some point in your life, so they're worth understanding.

State Surprise! You might have been surprised to receive a *Form 1099* your state's franchise tax board. This is because any amount of state income tax refunded to you is subject to federal tax in the following year. You are hearing this correctly—your state income tax refund is taxable at the federal level. In all fairness, you did receive a federal deduction for state taxes paid the prior year, so it could be a wash but, the 1099 might still come as a shock. If you are receiving large state refunds, consider adjusting your withholdings to avoid a short-term loan to the government.

Mortgage Myth. Despite popular belief, not all mortgage interest is deductible. Interest is only deductible on the first $1 million of borrowed funds used to buy, build, or improve a home. So, if you purchase a home for more than $1.25 million and put 20% down, you will not be able to deduct all your interest payments. Additionally, interest paid on an equity line used for purposes *other than* to buy, build, or improve your house, is only deductible on the first $100,000.

Add More Tax. An easy way to remember what alternative minimum tax (AMT) means is to think, add more tax. Simply put, AMT is an alternative "equation" to calculate your income tax liability. If this second way of doing math ends in a larger tax liability, then you will pay more. A few things that could potentially trigger AMT include unreimbursed business expenses, property taxes, state income taxes, and incentive stock options. If you really want to see if you've fallen into the AMT trap, check line 45 of your Form 1040.

Underpay and Pay. It's no surprise that the IRS wants your money, and it wants it now (or at least on time). If you do not withhold enough tax throughout the year, you could be subject to an underpayment penalty when you file. For most people, payroll withholdings facilitated by an employer will be sufficient. For the self-employed, retirees who are not collecting a paycheck, or workers with other substantial sources of income, however, it is your responsibility to make timely estimated tax payments.

End of Chapter Resources

Sample IRS Form 1040

To access the end of chapter resources, go to
www.GetTheSense.com/Book-Resources.

Glossary of Terms

Making Sense of It All

501(c)(3): A type of charitable organization that is qualified in the eyes of the IRS. After meeting certain IRS guidelines, contributions made to such charities may be tax-deductible and tax-free to the charity. Most well-known public charities are organized under IRC § 501(c)(3). (Entry #18)

529 College Savings Plan: An investment account used to earmark funds for college. Funds invested in a 529 account grow tax-free if used for college expenses, including tuition and room and board. Funds withdrawn that are not applied to college costs are subject to income tax and a 10% tax penalty on earnings. While contributions to a 529 plan are not federally tax-deductible, certain states allow contributions by residents to be deductible at the state level. (Entry #20)

Activities of Daily Living (ADLs): Routine activities that determine whether an insured qualifies to go on claim from a long-term care insurance policy. There are six basic ADLs: eating, bathing, dressing, toileting, transferring, and continence. A person's inability to perform two or more of the six ADLs will qualify them to receive benefits from their policy. (Entry #44)

Adjusted Gross Income (AGI): Total income subject to income tax (for example, wages, investment income, alimony, rental income) adjusted, or rather reduced, by certain deductions. Although AGI is not the number to which tax is actually applied, it does determine a taxpayer's eligibility to take certain deductions, or to use exemptions (for example, the Lifetime Learning Credit and student loan interest). AGI is found on line 37 and 38 of Form 1040. (Entry #54)

Amortize: The process in which a mortgage or loan is repaid over a set time period with fixed payments that include an amount to pay towards both principal and interest. The interest and principal portion of each payment of a fully amortized loan decrease and increase, respectively, over the course of the loan. The loan will be fully paid back at the end of the set period. (Entry #15)

Asset Allocation: The mix of investment types within a portfolio (i.e., stocks, bonds, and cash). The appropriate mix for an investor is determined by the individual's timeframe, risk tolerance, and financial situation. (Entry #30)

Benchmark: A standard used to measure the performance of an invested portfolio. Depending on the types of investments included in the strategy to be evaluated, a benchmark may be comprised of a single index like the S&P 500 or a combination of indices, like 60% S&P 500, 40% Dow Jones Industrial Average.

Benchmarks are a way to help investors put performance into perspective.

Bonds: A loan to corporations or governments in exchange for a fixed interest payment until maturity. Bonds are also referred to as "fixed income." The borrower pays a stated interest payment to the bondholder (investor) until it matures, and at maturity the company pays back all the money borrowed to the bondholder. (Entry #36)

Broker-Dealer: A firm that buys and sells securities (investments) on its own account as a principal before selling the securities to customers.

Budget: An estimation of income and expenses over a specified future period of time, typically monthly, that categorizes expenses and sets a spending goal. (Entry #1)

Custodian: A financial institution that holds securities (investments) for an investor's safekeeping. Think of a custodian like a valet service for your car. Investments are "parked" with a custodian. Charles Schwab, Fidelity Investments, and TD Ameritrade are all examples of custodians. (Entry #33)

Dependents: In the context of the IRS, a qualifying child or relative. The dependent must be your son, daughter, stepchild, foster child, brother, sister, half-brother, half-sister, stepbrother, stepsister, or a descendant of any of them. The dependent must be (a) younger than the taxpayer, must be (b) under age 19 at the end of the year, (c) under age 24 at the end of the year, a student, and younger than you (or your spouse, if filing jointly), or (d) any age if permanently and totally disabled. They must have lived with you for more than half of the year. The child must not have provided more than half of his or her own support for the year. They must not file a joint return for the year (unless that return is filed only to get a refund of income tax withheld or estimated tax paid). (Entry #54)

Discretionary Income: Discretionary income is the amount of an individual's income that is left for spending, investing, or saving after paying taxes and for personal necessities, such as food, a housing and transportation. The amount spent on luxury items and services, and vacations comes from your discretionary income. (Entry #10)

Dividend: A distribution of company profits (or reserves) to its shareholders. Dividends are generally paid quarterly.

Dollar Cost Averaging: The process of making regular recurring purchases of a particular investment, with a set dollar amount, regardless of the share price (for example, buying $500 of ABC Company stock on the 15th of every month). Since the purchase amount is fixed, more shares will be purchased when the stock price is lower and fewer shares will be purchased when the stock price is higher. Dollar cost averaging is a way of reducing the risk of buying into an investment all at once and at a single price.

Donor-Advised Fund (DAF): An investment account that is created specifically and solely for charitable donations. A DAF allows the donors to take a charitable deduction for the full amount of the contribution in the year of the contribution but delay actual donations to charity until a later date. (Entry #18)

Effective Tax Rate: The average rate at which an individual or corporation is taxed. To calculate the effective tax rate, divide total tax by taxable income. (Entry #53)

Emergency Fund: Cash set aside in a savings account to be used in the event of a personal financial catastrophe such as the loss of a job, a debilitating illness or a major unexpected expense. The purpose of the fund is to improve financial security by eliminating the need to incur credit card or other high interest debt options when unexpected expenses occur. (Entry #2)

Emerging Markets: Economies undertaking reforms and developments that will put them in the global scene. In other words, they are transitioning from a closed economy to an open one. Emerging markets are also categorized as having low relative income per capita (per person). There are a number of emerging economies in the world, the most noted of which are China, Brazil, Russia, and India.

Exchange Traded Fund (ETF): A marketable security (investment) that mimics an index. Unlike mutual funds, an ETF trades like a common stock on a stock exchange. ETFs experience price changes throughout the day as they are bought and sold. ETFs typically have higher daily liquidity and lower fees than mutual fund shares, making them an attractive alternative for individual investors. Because it trades like a stock, an ETF does not have its net asset value (NAV) calculated once at the end of every day like a mutual fund does. (Entry #35)

Exclusive Provider Organization (EPOs): A type of health insurance that combines the flexibility of PPO plans with the cost-savings of HMO plans. Insurers do not need to choose a primary care physician, and don't need referrals to see a specialist. However, care must be provided by doctors and hospitals within the EPO network. EPO plans don't cover care outside your network unless it's an emergency. (Entry #45)

Expense Ratio: The annual cost of a mutual fund, which pays for operational items such as the investment manager/advisor, record-keeping, tax preparation, legal expenses and auditing fees. Daily mutual fund values are expressed as "Net Asset Value" or NAV, which is the total value of the underlying investments, minus one day's worth of expenses. (Entry #34)

Fed Funds Rate: The interest rate paid for overnight lending between large, creditworthy institutions. The Fed Funds Rate is the starting rate that determines all other interest rates in the

U.S. (for example, mortgage rates). Think of it as the floor rate paid by those with the very best credit ratings for very short-term lending. Consumer rates will increase from this base rate based on credit standing and/or desired length of financing.

FICO Score: a statistical number that determines the likelihood that an individual will pay debts. FICO scoring is used by employers, lenders, insurance providers, landlords, cell phone providers, and certain utilities to decide whether to make loans to or do business with someone. A high number tells viewers that someone is fiscally responsible. (Entry #6)

Fiduciary Standard of Care: Requires certain financial advisors that are regulated by the Securities and Exchange Commission (SEC) to act solely in the best interest of a client when offering financial advice. (Entry #33)

Flexible Spending Account (FSA): An employer-provided benefit that allows employees to set aside up to $2,550 annually to be used for approved medical expenses throughout the year. The benefit of a FSA is that contributions and funds used are tax-free. Funds not used are lost. Depending on the plan, one of two options will exist to help use the funds: 1) carry over up to $500 of unused funds contributed to cover expenses in the following year (think of them like rollover minutes) and funds in excess of $500 will be forfeited, or 2) use the balance in the FSA account by March 15th of the following year or it will be forfeited. (Entry #45)

Form 1099: A tax form that reports the year-end summary of all non-employee income to the IRS. Four of the most common types of income reported on Form 1099 are: Dividends (1099-DIV), a stock or mutual fund that pays dividends; Interest Income (1099-INT), a checking, savings or other bank account that earns interest; Miscellaneous Income (1099-MISC), earned $600 or more working for someone as an independent contractor or if you're self-employed; or Retirement Plan Distributions (1099-R), receive $10 or more in distributions from pensions, annuities, profit-sharing plans, IRAs, etc. (Entry #56)

Gross Domestic Product (GDP): Is the value of all goods and services produced in a country. GDP may be calculated in different ways; the most common approach tallies consumer and government spending, business expenditures, and net exports (total exports minus imports) to arrive at GDP. GDP is an indicator of the productivity of a nation over a certain period of time.

Guaranteed Auto Protection (GAP) Insurance: Provides income for the insured when there is a difference between the determined actual cash value of a vehicle and the balance of the car loan (or lease) after a car accident. GAP coverage is typically only used on new cars purchased with a loan. GAP insurance is necessary if a car is involved in an accident and the insurance company decides the vehicle is totaled, and collision coverage will only pay the current market value, which is usually less than the amount still owed. (Entry #39)

Health Savings Account (HSA): A type of savings account that allows individuals enrolled in a high-deductible health plan (HDHP) to set aside funds for out-of-pocket medical expenses on a pre-tax basis. In 2017, the HSA funding limit is $3,400 for individuals and $6,750 for families (plus a $1,000 catch-up for participants age 55 or older). Interest and earnings on HSA funds grow tax-deferred and can be withdrawn tax-free if used for qualified medical expenses. Unlike FSAs, HSA funds may continue to accumulate if not spent. (Entry #45)

Irrevocable Trust: Is a document that can be created during life, or at death, that cannot be changed after it is created. The parties consist of a grantor (who gifts the assets), a trustee, and a beneficiary. Once the grantor establishes the irrevocable trust and transfers assets to it, it cannot be modified or terminated without the permission of the beneficiary and the grantor relinquishes all ownership of the assets in the trust. Irrevocable trusts are primarily established for the benefit of children or grandchildren to minimize estate tax and gift tax liabilities. (Entry #50)

LIBOR: An average of interest rates paid by banks in the London interbank market for short-term financing. LIBOR serves as a benchmark rate for many forms of financing, most commonly interest only mortgages, margin loans, and adjustable rate loans. Actual consumer rates will vary depending on a number of factors but will generally be LIBOR plus an additional amount (referred to as a spread). LIBOR stands for the London Interbank Offered Rate. (Entry #15)

Living Trust: A written agreement between a grantor (creator and funder of the trust), a trustee (responsible party of the trust), and a beneficiary (benefits from the property transferred to the trust). Unlike an irrevocable trust, living trusts are used to communicate the grantor's wishes related to managing or transferring property after the grantor's death or incapacity. Accordingly, the grantor, trustee and beneficiary are the same person during the grantor's life. A living trust can be modified during the grantor's life and is used to avoid probate. (Entry #46)

Marginal Income Tax Rate: The percentage of tax due on an additional dollar of income. The United States uses a bracket system of taxation, with each bracket having a different rate (percentage) of tax. The amount of income in each bracket changes annually. The marginal income tax rate is the rate that applies to the bracket that an additional dollar of income falls into. (Entry #52)

Market Capitalization (Market-Cap): The total dollar value of a company's stock in the open market. Market capitalization (often referred to as "market cap") is determined by multiplying the share price of a stock by the number of shares outstanding.

Definitions vary, but the approximate market cap of mid-sized companies is between $2 billion and $10 billion; companies whose cap size is larger are considered "large-cap" and those that are smaller are "small-cap." (Entry #35)

Modified Adjusted Gross Income (MAGI): A calculation of income that is used to determine an individual's eligibility for various federal tax benefits. Most notably, it is used to determine how much of an individual's IRA contribution is deductible, the amount of Medicare premiums and surtax, and whether an individual is eligible for certain tax credits. To calculate MAGI, start with your AGI and add to it nontaxable income, deductions for IRA contributions, student loan interest deductions, tuition and fees and interest from EE savings bonds used to pay higher education expenses. (Entry #27)

Mutual Fund: An investment vehicle that comprises a pool of underlying investments, such as stocks, bonds, commodities, currencies, or a combination of investment types, selected by a professional manager. The underlying investments may be selected to track the performance of an index (known as index or passive funds) or they may be selected at the manager's discretion (known as active funds). Investments within an index fund are changed only when the tracking index changes, whereas active fund investment changes may be made at any time—again at the manager's discretion. A mutual fund is divided into shares that are owned by investors who share proportionally in the underlying investment returns. Mutual fund trades are processed at the end of the trading day and pricing is based on the closing value of the underlying investments. (Entry #35)

Point of Service (POS): A type of health insurance plan that has features similar to both HMO and PPO plans. Similar to a PPO, care can be sought from in-network or out-of-network providers, but very little benefit will be provided towards care outside of the network. Like HMOs, some plans require the insured party to be seen by a primary care physician before being seen by a specialist or receiving out-of-network care. (Entry #45)

Probate: A public legal process in which a court determines the validity of a deceased person's will. Probate also includes the administration of a deceased person's estate by the appointed executor (named in the will) or an administrator (named by the court in absence of a will). Estate administration includes collecting assets, paying liabilities and taxes, and distributing property to heirs. In many states, the probate process is long and expensive. (Entry #46)

Qualified Domestic Relations Order (QDRO): A court order that explains how a retirement pension or account that has been earned during marriage will be split up following divorce. A QDRO provides a legal right of an ex-spouse to receive a portion of a retirement plan account or benefit payments, effectively establishing them as a co-beneficiary. Such documentation helps ensure that the transfer of retirement assets to an ex-spouse is not subject to income tax. (Entry #17)

Registered Investment Advisor (RIA): Is an investment management firm that is registered with the Securities and Exchange Commission (SEC) and/or state securities authorities and is legally obligated to act in the best interest of their clients. This fiduciary duty was initially unique to RIA advisory firms. RIA firms are compensated on a percentage basis of their assets under management, as opposed to brokerage firms who are compensated on commissions and sales commissions.

Rider: An added provision to an insurance policy that provides additional benefits to the policyholder at an additional cost. Standard policies usually don't cover expensive items or additional people, so riders should be added where needed to provide additional coverage. (Entry #40)

Sharpe Ratio: A measure of an investment's performance that takes into account the investment's level of risk. Sharpe ratio helps to assess the extent to which an investment's returns have been generated by taking risk. The higher the ratio, the better performance has been on a risk-adjusted basis. (Entry #30)

Standard Deviation: A measure of an investment's volatility, specifically the variance of returns around its average return. Understanding an investment's volatility is important to determine if it is appropriate for an investor's risk tolerance or financial situation. Standard deviation is a measure of price volatility and should not be interpreted as risk of loss on an investment. (Entry #30)

Stock: An investment in a corporation in exchange for an ownership interest, including rights to assets or earnings. Stocks may be purchased on a public exchange or, if the corporation is not publicly traded, received by private placement. (Entry #36)

Successor Trustee: An individual (or company) that assumes the responsibilities of a trustee once the initial trustee passes away or becomes unable to act. Like the initial trustee, a successor trustee is liable for ensuring that all property in the trust is held or distributed to the beneficiaries, in accordance with the terms of the trust. Successor trustees have a fiduciary duty to act in the best interest of trust beneficiaries when overseeing property owned by the trust. (Entry #50)

Taxable Income: The amount of income used to calculate the tax due and is found on line 43 of Form 1040. Taxable income is total income (line 22 on Form 1040) less allowable deductions and exemptions. (Entry #52)

Term Life Insurance: A type of life insurance that remains in force for a set term, most commonly 10, 15, 20, or 30 years. If the insured passes away within the coverage period, the beneficiaries receive a payout called the death benefit. The set coverage period makes term insurance cheaper than permanent policies that provide coverage throughout an insured's entire life (regardless of length). (Entry #4)

Trustee: An individual (or company) named in the trust that is responsible and liable for ensuring that all property in the name of the trust is held or distributed to the named beneficiaries, in accordance with the terms of the trust. Trustees have a fiduciary duty to act in the best interest of trust beneficiaries when overseeing property owned by the trust. For living trusts, most commonly the creators of the trust are the initial trustees. (Entry #50)

Sources

Appleby, Denise. "Designating a Trust as Retirement Beneficiary."
Investopedia. Accessed September 6, 2017.
http://www.investopedia.com/articles/retirement/04/081804.asp

Blankenship, Jim. "Understanding the Underpayment Penalty
and How to Avoid It." *Forbes*, June 25, 2012,
http://www.forbes.com/sites/advisor/2012/06/25/
understanding-the-underpayment-penalty-and-how-to-
avoid-it/#78914e8958c6

Carnevale, Anthony P., Ban Cheah, and Andrew R. Hanson. "The
Economic Value of College Majors." Georgetown University,
2015.
https://cew.georgetown.edu/cew-reports/
valueofcollegemajors/

Federal Trade Commission (FTC). "Lost or Stolen Credit, ATM,
and Debit Cards." August 2012. Accessed September 6, 2017.
https://www.consumer.ftc.gov/articles/0213-lost-or-stolen-
credit-atm-and-debit-cards

Fidelity Viewpoints. "How Much Do I Need to Save for
    Retirement?" June 5, 2017,
    https://www.fidelity.com/viewpoints/retirement/how-much-
    money-do-i-need-to-retire

Insurance Information Institute. "Understanding Your Insurance
    Deductible." Accessed September 6, 2017.
    http://www.iii.org/article/understanding-your-insurance-
    deductible

Internal Revenue Service (IRS). "Are You Covered by an
    Employer's Retirement Plan?" Last modified August 17, 2017,
    https://www.irs.gov/retirement-plans/are-you-covered-by-an
    -employers-retirement-plan

IRS. "Eight Tips for Deducting Charitable Contributions." March
    22, 2011. Accessed September 6, 2017.
    https://www.irs.gov/uac/eight-tips-for-deducting-charitable-
    contributions

Personal Spending Worksheet, Sample Credit Report
    Dispute Letter of Explanation (http://www.myfico.com/
    crediteducation/rights/sample-credit-report-dispute-letter-
    of-explanation.aspx)

Piferi, Rachel L., and Kathleen Lawler. "Social Support
    and Ambulatory Blood Pressure: An Examination of
    Both Receiving and Giving." *International Journal of*

Psychophysiology 62, no. 2 (Nov. 2006): 328-336.
http://www.sciencedirect.com/science/article/pii/
S0167876006001917

Savingforcollege.com. "529 Plans: Which Expenses Are Qualified?
(Script)." August 1, 2011,
http://www.savingforcollege.com/questions-answers/article.
php?article_id=130

TurboTax. "What Is the Difference between AGI and MAGI on
Your Taxes?" Updated for tax year 2016,
https://turbotax.intuit.com/tax-tools/tax-tips/IRS-Tax-Return
/What-Is-the-Difference-Between-AGI-and-MAGI-on-Your-
Taxes-/INF22699.html

United States Department of Labor. "QDRO's - An Overview
FAQs." Accessed September 6, 2017.
https://www.dol.gov/ebsa/faqs/faq_qdro.html

Walsh, Colleen. "Money Spent on Others Can Buy Happiness."
Harvard Gazette. April 17, 2008.
http://news.harvard.edu/gazette/story/2008/04/money-spent-
on-others-can-buy-happiness/

Made in the USA
Columbia, SC
11 February 2018